Peeing Uphill

and Other Backpacking Wisdom

Jeffrey Probst

Peeing Uphill and Other Backpacking Wisdom

Published by Outland Publishing.
Assisted by CreateSpace, an Amazon company.

Email: outlandpub@yahoo.com

Introduction

Backpacking is fresh! It always will be. Everything about it is new and robust. The air, the earth, the wildlife, the scenery, the adventure, the changing seasons, and even a person's attitude are keenly attuned by backpacking. No matter the weather, backpacking always feels as fresh as a cool breeze ushering out a thunderstorm.

Looking for a gratifying outdoor sport? Backpacking just might be the best available. Its rewards are numerous, ranging from personal achievement to unmatched scenic exhibits. Performed properly backpacking can leave you feeling confident, satisfied, and mentally refreshed. If done haphazardly, you might feel tired, sore, and discouraged, and vow to *never* do it again. The first goal of this book is to illustrate simple and healthy ways to backpack.

Backpacking is not a precise science, but rather an art that can be enjoyed using your own unique style. Hopefully, this book will help you develop that style, by suggesting many resourceful pointers. The philosophy preached here is "less is better." Less weight and less expense have payoffs that are easily recognized.

Having backpacked for over twenty years, I have experimented with many alternatives for equipment, food, clothing, and activities. Much has been learned by observing and chatting with fellow hikers. This book's second objective is to present choices that make backpacking affordable on most any income. You may have the impression that backpacking is an expensive sport, and shouldn't be attempted without the latest ultra-light gear. This couldn't be further from the truth. Some of my fondest memories are of adventures attempted as a teenager, when I could barely afford my share of the gasoline to get to the trailhead. Needless to say, each of us learned to improvise. Part of the excitement of each trip was figuring out new ways to substitute household items for the things we were *supposed* to have. I still use many of these substitutes in favor of the more expensive gear so often suggested.

Originally, I thought about calling this book "Backpacking Made Easy, Made Cheap." But then I realized there's not much easy about it. In fact, "easy backpacking" is somewhat of an oxymoron, like "military intelligence," or "committee decision." On the other hand, backpacking does not have to be difficult either. Physical exertion and discomfort can be minimized by sensible planning. Then, enhance your knowledge with a little backwoods savvy, and your outings will be easier; but never easy.

As an added bonus, this book features two chapters on subjects not often addressed by other backpacking publications. A chapter on "what not to take" can save you many *killer* pounds if you heed the sound advice found there. It will even tell you why some things might be better off left behind. But don't feel too guilty if you still pack some of the gear I shun. We all have things we like to splurge on.

Another special and unique chapter explains how to catch high country trout, even for novice fishermen. Learn the secrets of catching finicky alpine fish. I'll not only tell you how to fish, but when and where. Different methods are explained for angling in lakes, streams and beaver dams. Hooking your share of backwoods trout is often quite easy, once you learn the rules they play by.

To increase your free time, many work saving tips for camping and hiking are given. Who wants to spend time working when they could be pursuing their favorite interests or just relaxing? By practicing proper trail techniques, and knowing how to choose a wilderness camp, many of the discomforts of backpacking can be alleviated.

So, whether you're a greenhorn or an old-timer, rich or poor, homely or handsome; just grab yer pack, grub, gear and bedroll, and let's discover a pastime you'll love—backpacking!

Who knows? You might even learn how to pee uphill.

Table of Contents

1

Why Go?

People often ask the question, "Why do you go backpacking? It sounds like a lot of work." Well, I'll readily admit it does involve much more physical exertion than roadside camping, and there are few creature comforts in the back country. But despite these drawbacks, the advantages far outweigh the extra effort required to really escape the rat-race. My sister insists that I like to go backpacking, "because you get to pee outside."

Review the pluses, and see which ones peak your interest enough to give backpacking a try. You probably already know several good reasons, and it's likely you'll realize some new ones. Why go? Let's find out.

Everyone that undertakes backpacking has their own favorite reason. Perhaps the most common is solitude. Even though the sport has grown in popularity, there is still ample space for everyone. You should be able to be alone, even in high use areas. It's great to get away by yourself, with magnificent surroundings. It gives you a chance to think about things you normally wouldn't. Mental relaxation can be yours.

For centuries, great thinkers and philosophers have sought out places to be alone. Find peace and quiet, and problem solving is easier. Meditating in the grandeur of the wilderness may help you put problems into their proper perspective. People naturally seek out quiet, peaceful surroundings when they need to relax or ponder meaningful subjects. The backcountry, with its wide expanses of natural beauty and serenity, is highly addictive to solitude seekers.

Maybe you like to be uncrowded for reasons other than meditation. How good would it make you feel to have an isolated lake all to yourself? Elbow room to fish and camp is a priceless commodity. You can *let loose* without worrying or wondering who's watching, or what someone else might think. Not only does no one bother you, but you don't bother anyone else. Should your path cross with other packers, some unspoken rules of common courtesy (covered later) make backpacking a pleasant experience for all.

Freedom to go where you want, and do what you want, is a luxury most of us lack in our everyday lives. In the backcountry, you don't answer to anyone. There's no boss. You can eat, sleep, fish, hike, or goof off whenever you want. This all sounds pretty irresponsible (hooray), but you will have a different set of responsibilities. You will be tremendously responsible for yourself, your companions, and the way you treat the environment.

Physical fitness crazes have made backpacking and hiking increasingly popular. For some, hiking is the finest part of a wilderness trek, while others see it as a necessary evil to get the rewards at the trail's end. It does feel good to stretch and hike, but like any other exercise, don't overdo it. Learn to enjoy walking, and know your limits before planning any trip. Exercise makes one feel good, but over exertion only makes a person sore or sick. The chapter about trail techniques will demonstrate ways to enjoy hiking with minimal huffing and puffing.

Before we get too far along, let me introduce Bradley, my *little* brother. At least he used to be little. Now, half a foot taller than me, I have to settle for *younger* brother. We've backpacked together for many years, and despite our differing life-styles, we have found the wilderness to be something special to us both. Throughout this book, Bradley offers little bits of woodsy wit and wisdom. Being the rebellious and rough guy he is, I suggest taking his suggestions with a grain of salt, or maybe with your tongue in cheek. I always enjoy Bradley's company, and feel safer when he's around. With him nearby, I'll never be the highest point during a lightning storm.

Bradley's reason for backpacking is to "get away from people, the cops, and work." Personally, I think he mostly enjoys the great companionship. Well enough sidetracking for now, let's get back to the finer things of life. More from Bradley later.

When backpacking is mentioned, what picture comes to your mind? Most likely it will be of peaceful lakes and streams surrounded by local flora, or maybe majestic mountains claim the scene. Whatever you envision, it is probably beautiful, colorful, and pleasing to the eye. Fantastic scenery magnifies the amount of pleasure of any kind of trip. In the backcountry it is abundant. Panoramic views of nature have always recharged the spiritual and mental batteries of man. Perhaps this is why spectacular scenery ranks high on the list of reasons to pack it in.

Visionary treats await hikers as they venture into the wilderness. Nature unveils her entire spectrum. There is everything from vistas viewed from mountain tops to the simple beauty of a wildflower adorned by a bumblebee. Nature puts on spectacular shows. You'll enjoy a front row seat to amazing sunrises, sunsets, thundershowers, waterfalls, reflective lakes, stately peaks, bright green meadows, and the countless antics of wildlife.

Sight is not the only sense that receives extra stimulation. Listening to a babbling brook, the wind in the trees, or the tune of a Rocky Mountain jay can be tranquilizing. Pleasing sounds soothe our emotions like mellow music.

No longer shielded from nature, you'll experience the warmth of the sun, the cool air of the night, the wind, the rain, cold spring water, and muscles not often used. What we feel largely determines how we feel, so bring along some rain gear to keep you dry, cozy, and happy when nasty weather threatens to dampen your spirits.

There's something about backpacking that wakes up taste buds too. And if you savor eating as much as I do, that's good news. All food tastes better on a backpacking trip than it does at home. This is largely due to increased appetites and the fine surroundings. What better atmosphere could you ask for? Who can resist the smell of bacon or fresh trout frying for breakfast? Add some crisp hash-browns and, well . . . we'll discuss menus later.

Another reason for backpacking might be the challenges. Because it's there (an old but somehow meaningful cliche). What are you made of? How far can you go? How little can you get by on? There is an long-standing oriental belief that a man is measured by how little he can get by with, not by how much he has obtained. In the wilds there are many opportunities to prove yourself, and work toward personal goals. It is a very satisfying feeling to be able to coexist comfortably with nature for several days, with just thirty pounds of provisions. Facing the challenges of nature may sometimes be just an illusion of grandeur on our part, but it is a rewarding illusion.

Perhaps you'll find that special spot—an almost spiritual place where you feel like part of the earth, like you were meant to be there. It may be a singular view point, a lake, a trail, or an entire mountain range. When you discover yours, you'll know. Just being there makes you feel in touch with something serene and powerful, removed from the complex lifestyles of man. Just knowing that such a place exists helps you develop an inner peace and a hope; a hope that you can return to feast upon its spirit.

Outdoor hobbies may lure you to the backwoods. Photography subjects are unlimited! Whether you prefer close-ups of wildflowers or animals, panormas of mountain ranges, or just snapshots for lasting memories, there is constant opportunity. You'll be seeing the land during all times of the day and all kinds of weather. Keep your camera handy. You never know when that once-in-a-lifetime photo will appear.

Fishing in primitive lakes, ponds, and streams is always exciting because you never know what to expect. One lake might yield fifty small brookies in a few hours, another a couple of large cutthroats, while yet another may provide nothing but aesthetics. If you discover one lake doesn't fill the frying pan, try a different one. There is often another lake nearby that will. Choosing the right lure has always been part of the thrill of fishing. In the backcountry a new element of angling pleasure comes into play—finding the right lake or stream.

One final argument for trying a wilderness experience with backpacks is that of discovery and adventure. When planning a trip, try to pick a place you haven't been to before. Around each bend awaits a new surprise. The surprise may be anything from a cold cascading waterfall, to a photogenic bull moose. Lakes and mountains seen for the first time offer many exciting activities and camping memories. The anticipation and excitement of your group amplifies whenever a new section of the wilderness is chosen for an excursion.

After trying several new places you will be tempted to return to some of them. Do it! If an area was just the way you liked it, then definitely return. You probably weren't given the chance to fully explore it the first time. There is seldom enough time to do everything you want to. Going back is an excellent way to get the extra time you need.

Inside every adult is a little child. Inside every child is an endless supply of adventurous daydreams. Packing-in gives us a rare chance to live some of the expeditions we fantasize about. You don't have to be young to desire adventure, and certainly not to participate in one. Perhaps you have the characteristic that is found in every great explorer, curiosity.

So, the first thing you need to do is dream; then decide what kind of adventure you want in the wilderness. Chances are good that backpacking provides a means to fulfill your desires. Know why you want to go. Maybe for the solitude, or exercise, or scenery, or fishing, or photography, or the challenge of it all. These are the reasons most commonly given. Hopefully, you have thought of some others. Give backpacking a try, but beware, it can be extremely habit forming, and good for your health. And besides, it's damn fun.

2

Preparations & Getting Hyped

Preparations for a backpacking trip can be as elaborate and detailed as you care to make them, but should at least be sufficient to assure a successful experience. In this chapter are guidelines you might follow to be sure all the bases are covered before beginning your trek. You may not need all of these suggestions, depending on how far you travel, the size of your party, and the length of your stay; but until you have been on several backpacking trips, it may be a good idea to review this chapter before making definite plans. If nothing else, planning serves as a booster for getting *psyched* about an upcoming adventure.

ORGANIZE

Each excursion usually begins with someone organizing it. Generally, it is advisable to have one person in charge of coordinating the planning.

Anyone wishing to join the group must meet with the approval of the rest of the party to assure that there will not be too many going along. This is an important factor to many backpackers. Good group sizes range from three to eight hikers. More than eight may be too slow to move, hard to manage, or too big of an ecological burden on a campsite. Less than three could be dangerous in an emergency situation.

SET THE DATE

This may actually be the first step. Some trips are scheduled months in advance so everyone can arrange time away. Having a date set makes it easier to add others to the group if you wish. If someone wishes to come along you are able to tell them when and possibly where you are going. Be sure to write it on the calendar so that no other plans are made during that time.

Avoid a last minute cancellation, as it will most likely upset the arrangements of others. If you drop out, do it early enough that the remaining party can ask someone else to go.

CHOOSE AN AREA AND ROUTE

Decide where you are going as soon as possible, and involve as many of the group as possible in this decision. Then everyone will have a chance to review maps and become familiar with the area. Make it known how long and steep the trail is. The difficulty of the hike is a determining factor. Other considerations might be availability of drinking water, type of terrain, fishing prospects, campsites, and accessibility.

In figuring how far and fast your party can hike, base the decision on the weakest member. Be conservative with this estimate. Hiking slows considerably at high elevations, going uphill, with a full pack. You don't want to be exhausted upon reaching your destination, as you will need enough energy to setup camp.

After choosing the area to visit, map out the route you'll be hiking. Then everyone will at least know the starting point and destination of the hike, and how many miles in between.

Here's a nifty idea if you want to plan a hike that begins at one trailhead and ends at another. Split your group into two parties. One starts at point A, the other at point B. When the two parties meet on the trail, exchange car keys and continue on. This system also works with just one car by dropping off the first party at point A, then the others drive to point B. When the two parties meet, the second party gives the keys to the first, who upon reaching point B will drive back to point A to pick up the second party.

RESTRICTIONS AND LAWS

After selecting a site for a backpacking adventure, find out the laws and restrictions for that area. Review the fishing limits and regulations. Many waters are restricted to flies or artificial lures, or have special limits.

Some wilderness areas require a permit for hiking or backpacking. If this is the case, reservations may have to be made, so allow for plenty of advance notice. Also, find out if fires are allowed, or a fire permit is required.

If you are going during a hunting season, some types of firearms are prohibited. Very few hikers carry guns, but if you do, know the laws for carrying one.

PETS

Many wilderness areas prohibit dogs. All national parks do. If dogs are permitted where you are going, get permission from your group before bringing a dog, and be aware of all the disadvantages of canines in the backcountry. I have seen dogs noisily defend "their" territory, steal my food, crap in camp, crap on the trail, spook horses, fight other dogs, growl at hikers, and chase big game. Now I'm not saying you should or shouldn't bring old Duke along, but unless the hound is extremely well trained, and you want to tie it up at night, I'm inclined to leave dogs home.

If you do take the dog, then properly condition him. He needs extensive walks on pavement and trails to toughen his pads. The backcountry trails are loaded with rocks and dirt, and while pavement is not the same, it's the next best thing. If your dog's pads are not conditioned, then leave him home. Otherwise you might be carrying him when his feet become too sore to travel.

PHYSICAL CONDITIONING

Walking, walking, and walking are probably the three best exercises to ready yourself for hiking. Wilderness trails are seldom level, so if possible, workout where you can walk uphill and down. Periodically, practice hiking with boots on. Not only will legs be strengthened, you may be able to break in stiff boots or spot a footwear problem before it's too late.

Now what do I mean by *walking*? Mention walking to five different people, and you'll likely get five different interpretations. You may think you know how to walk, after all you've done it since you were a toddler. But what I'm talking about is a fast-paced walk, with long strides. Put some spring in your step, and do it for at least a half hour.

Walk regularly several months prior to a backcountry trek. The key word is *regularly*. A couple of weeks before, take a hike in similar terrain. This is also an excellent chance to check gear before getting too far from home.

Calf muscles are often the first to tire. Strengthen calves by a simple exercise that can be done on a single step at home. Stand on the step with the balls of your feet on the edge of the step. Raise up on your toes, then lower yourself until your heels are extended as far below the lip of the step as possible without discomfort. Start out with about fifteen repetitions, and see if you can work your way up to easily completing a set of forty reps.

Calisthenics for the neck and shoulders are valuable too. These areas receive a lot of stress on a long hike. Wearing a weighted pack during your regular workout is the best way to introduce muscles to the extra load they will be required to carry.

If you are not in great shape, and do not have time to become so, you can still go. Just be sure to make the hike short with minimal uphill slopes. If you have doubts about your fitness, consult a doctor to determine if backpacking is safe for you.

During the week before a long hike, taper down your exercise routine and eat lots of high carbohydrate foods. Doing so will build and conserve carbohydrate stores within muscles, which in turn will increase your endurance throughout a strenuous trek.

CONTENTS OF PACK

Know exactly what is needed so nothing extra weighs you down. Make a checklist of all pack contents and figure it's weight. A standard formula for the *most* a person should carry is one-fourth their own weight. This is a maximum, a suggested poundage might be less. Once a checklist is made, check each item to assure it will last the entire backpacking trip. Replace anything in question. Broken equipment can be a real hardship, miles into the wilderness.

Groups can divide gear between members to allow each one to carry less. Items to consider sharing are tents, pots, pans, food, ropes, first aid kits, sewing kits, and camp tools. Make arrangements for any shared items well in advance, and double check everything is packed before starting out. Imagine how you might feel when your partner says, "I thought you were bringing the salt."

CLIMATE AND WEATHER

The gear taken depends largely on the type of area you are packing in to. Will you need rain gear? Most often, yes. If much sun is expected, take along sunblock and sunglasses. Is mosquito repellent needed? What about a snake bite kit? Maybe salt tablets are needed to replace body minerals lost from sweating. Know what the environment will be like, then review the checklist to make sure it is adequate.

DRINKING WATER

Don't count on finding drinking water, especially while hiking. Start with a container of pure water from home. Once in the wilderness, purify all drinking water that you are not absolutely sure of. For me, that would be any water except spring water. Plan your equipment to fit the water needs of the situation. To be safe, a large covered aluminum pot for boiling water is suggested. If you're heading into desert country, take along emergency gear to construct a solar still.

MENUS

Jot down a menu for each meal, and don't take any more. The exception may be if the meal includes fresh fish you hope to catch. Have an entree to replace the fish if they're not biting. Also itemize snacks to avoid extra baggage. Returning home with any food means you carried it for the entire length of the trek for no reason, and ounces quickly become pounds after several trail miles.

TRANSPORTATION

"Whose car are we going to take?" This has always been a delicate subject between outdoorsmen, but don't procrastinate this decision. Unless four wheel drive is needed to get to the trailhead, any car or truck capable of hauling people and backpacks will do. Good etiquette for passengers who don't take their vehicles is to pay for the gas.

My long-legged brother Bradley suggests, "Don't overload your vehicle with people and gear. An uncomfortable ride can make an unpleasant trip." He obviously recalls the five hour ride he and I shared; stuffed in the back of a "Toyota Land Cruiser" along with four backpacks. I'll admit I was never so glad to get out of a car and start walking.

TRIP ITINERARY

The organizer should inform each member of the party well in advance where they will be staying each night of the trip, and what the daily activities are likely to include. Each person can then let their family know where they will be in case of an emergency.

PACKING

Everyone packs a little differently, and that's fine. However, there are a couple of good rules worth mentioning. Tie large heavy items (tents, sleeping bags) on top, while smaller heavy gear should be inside the pack as close to the middle of your back as possible. This distributes the weight more evenly on the entire body. Pack items to be used first, last. Priority items will then be on top or in the side pockets.

TRIM TOENAILS

This seemingly tiny task is important for your comfort. Long nails can turn into blackened, ingrown, or lost nails. Ouch!

THE DAY BEFORE, EAT ENERGY

Hikers commonly eat a big meal the day before a trek to build up energy. What you eat is more important than how much. Carbohydrates are best since they can be stored by the body, and quickly turned into energy when needed the following day. Excellent meals the day before would consist of pasta such as spaghetti or lasagna, which are loaded with valuable carbohydrates.

Usually backpacking trips begin in the morning. Get plenty of sleep the night before, and have a light breakfast. Hiking on a full stomach will take extra effort, and may nauseate you.

Preparations have been outlined up until the last minute. The next several chapters will discuss the items you should and should not take, and can help you create a personalized checklist.

3

Get Yer Gear

Equipment in good repair is what you'll need. The latest backpacking gear from the local sporting goods store is not necessarily the answer. Although you can buy great gear, consider using things you might already have, or that cost less. Many substitutions can be made with little, if any, discomfort.

Good backpacking equipment is important, but equally important is a good mental attitude and mental toughness. Even with the best gear, you will still sacrifice many of the comforts of home. A few more comforts may be given up by using alternative equipment, but those concessions are small, especially when compared to the original sacrifice of forsaking the easy life, and heading to the backcountry. With the proper frame of mind, one can overcome most inconveniences, and enjoy the wilderness. On the other hand, a poor or mediocre attitude can easily lead to an unhappy camper, no matter how well he is outfitted. Bradley scowls, "Don't keep bitchen' and moaning 'cause I don't wanna hear it."

This chapter covers all of the equipment needed for backpacking, as well as popular optional items. Less expensive alternative gear will be mentioned whenever possible. Hopefully, these substitutions will lend insight into ways to save money and pack weight. This book organizes equipment into four logical groups to assist you with your planning. The four groups are: pocket items, individual items, group items, and optional equipment. Understanding these categories should help reduce weight and expenses, especially when group items are shared.

POCKET ITEMS:

The following items should be kept in your pockets while in the wilderness. With these few basics, you could survive until help arrives, should you become lost or injured without your pack.

WATERPROOF MATCHES

The ability to start a fire is of paramount importance when it comes to wilderness survival, and can be equally important for assuring a pleasurable backpacking trip. At the very least, you'll need a way to ignite a portable stove. Waterproof matches are a superior choice, and can be purchased or made. Simply melt a small amount of wax on the heads of some wooden kitchen matches. There are specially made containers to keep matches dry, or you could use an empty plastic aspirin bottle or an old 35mm film tube. Should you elect to buy waterproof matches, then also take along some plain matches. Use the plain matches when possible, saving the more expensive waterproof ones for an emergency. A box of waterproof matches can last for many years before they are actually needed.

Disposable lighters are often used since they can sustain a flame longer than a match, stay lit in a breeze, and are waterproof. If you use a lighter, be sure to also tote some waterproof matches in case the lighter fails.

KNIFE

For safety reasons, the knife of a backpacker should be of the folding variety. A long sheath knife has little purpose on a backpacking trip. The Swiss Army knife has long been recognized as one of the best multipurpose tools on the market, but any sharp folding knife will do. Whatever knife you select, be sure it is sharpened before your trek. Dull blades are frustrating, and more dangerous than sharp ones.

The most common uses for a knife will be notching or carving wood, shaving kindling, cutting rope, kitchen chores, and cleaning fish. Choose your blade sizes accordingly. If you should happen to get into a survival situation, your knife will be second in importance. Only matches rank higher.

COMPASS

A compass may save your life in a survival situation, or may prevent you from getting lost in the first place. For this reason it should be kept with you at all times. However, its most likely use will be to help you arrive at your destination by the quickest and safest route. There is no economical substitute for a compass, but they come in a wide price range from about three dollars to well over thirty. They all point north. Choose one that best suites your needs and pocketbook, and learn how to use it with a topographical map. For general backpacking, an inexpensive compass will suffice. Leave the more expensive models for people that require pinpoint accuracy for serious orienteering.

SNACKS

Quick energy is the main benefit of snacks. Don't keep all of your munchies in your pockets, but keep some there at all times, *just in case.* Excellent trail goodies include granola bars, raisins, nuts, gorp, and candy. Avoid chocolate (it melts) and gum. Chewing gum while hiking makes it more difficult to breath easily. Many hikers take along jerky or beef sticks for snacks. These will not provide the instant energy needed during a hike, so save them for lunch or until camp is reached.

I mentioned candy, but perhaps I shouldn't have. Refined sugar acts like a drug. It picks you up, but soon after lets you down. I like to eat candy when I really need a quick boost, such as having to climb a steep hill just before reaching camp. Once at camp, I don't care if the sugar lets me down.

Trail mix can be bought in a variety of combinations, or blend your own from nuts, dried fruits, granola, and small candies.

INDIVIDUAL ITEMS:
The next group of items are basic essentials that should be packed by each individual. Unless small children are going, everyone should carry their own.

THE PACK
Often referred to as the "house on your back," the pack should be chosen much like a house; keeping comfort and space in mind. There are two basic types of packs, internal and external. Each has its good and bad points.

The internal is the logical choice for mountaineering and skiing. It hugs your back closely and becomes a part of you. This results in better balance, which is critical to climbers. But more of us are backpackers than climbers. Because the internal fits so snug, your back will sweat profusely even during a cool day of hiking. A hot day can get *unbearable.* Other disadvantages are the price, and the fact that all gear, including sleeping bag, must be stuffed inside. I guess the latter reason could be considered an advantage if you're not cramped for space.

External frame packs come in a wide variety of styles, capacities, and sizes (for all sizes of people). Packs are attached to a metal frame. The frame is also used for tying on sleeping bags, pads, tents, fishing poles, and so on. The secret to finding the right pack for you is to *try on lots of packs.* Put in some heavy gear to get a feeling what it will be like with a full load.

There are two critical fittings on an external pack: 1) The hip belt should ride on the widest part of the hip to minimize pinching and maximize proper weight distribution. 2) Adjust the shoulder strap to a 45 degree angle from the pack frame to the shoulder. This assures pressure will be applied directly down, instead of tugging on neck and shoulder muscles.

SLEEPING BAG

A large portion of each person's day is spent sleeping. This is equally true while backpacking, so you'll want to be comfortable. Most likely, no matter what you take along won't be as comfy as your own bed, but you can make it acceptable. The sleeping bag is the most important part of the bedroll. It must be warm and roomy enough. Best bags will be filled with "Dacron" or down, with a rip-stop exterior. Down-filled are much more expensive, and are usually only needed for cold climates.

The mummy and the full-size bag are the two basic models. The main differences are: The mummy is more compact and light, but many people don't like the restricted feeling. The weight difference is often less than a pound, so most "happy campers" opt for a full-size bag. Regardless of the style, a liner makes a huge difference, when it comes to keeping warm all night.

There are not a lot of alternatives to a good sleeping bag. You could get by with a regular, bulky bag designed for roadside camping, if you don't mind the extra weight and can keep it dry. Maybe you don't have a sleeping bag at all. Don't let that keep you at home. You could make like an old-west cowboy, and use a couple of wool blankets. Of course, this should not be your first choice because of their awkwardness to pack and the extra pounds they heap upon you. On second thought, get a good sleeping bag.

PADDING

Gone are the days when a bed could be fashioned from fresh pine boughs or soft meadow grasses. Our wilderness today is too heavily used and too fragile for such rustic practices. It is entirely feasible however to enjoy a good night's sleep in the back country without harming the environment. Padding is necessary for warmth and to maintain a comfortable sleeping posture. Your choice is a simple one—either foam or a hybrid air/foam mattress.

If you select a foam pad, choose one that is lined to prevent moisture from soaking in it. Otherwise, you may have to dry out your pad daily. Determine if you need a full length pad, or if you can get by with a hip length pad. A full length is slightly heavier, but keeps feet off the cold ground.

The best choice is one of the many hybrids. These require only a few puffs of air to provide the right amount of cushion, and easily deflate for compact packing. Review the options, and try a "hands on" demo at an outdoor store.

WATER CONTAINER

Pure water is a necessity whether on the trail or in camp. The most popular ways to tote water are by canteen or water bottle. Use the one most convenient for you, and best fits your personal needs and activities.

Canteens come in a variety of shapes and sizes, and can be hung on the belt, pack, or shoulder while hiking. A large canteen doesn't weigh much more than a small one unless you fill it. This is a significant note, because you can take a large canteen containing just enough water for the trail, and when camp is reached, fill it up. With a large canteen, you'll make fewer trips to the waterhole.

Sturdy plastic water bottles are probably the easiest to pack. The tubular shape allows for a nice fit in the side pocket of a pack, permitting easy access while walking.

FLASHLIGHT

Artificial light on a wilderness trek is not needed in great abundance. Usage of a flashlight will likely consist of helping you get from the campfire to your bedroll, or aid you during the night should nature call. If this is the case, a reliable penlight using AA batteries will do nicely. Test the batteries before you go, and replace weak ones. Alkaline batteries may not seem like the cheapest choice, but they are in the long run. They may cost twice the price of regular batteries, but last many times longer. Unless the trip is longer than a week, there is no need to pack extra batteries.

On a budget? Try a disposable flashlight. It won't be as bright or long lasting, but it will do the job for a few days.

Want to turn your flashlight into an inexpensive lantern? Simply stand a flashlight on end, and slip a clear quart-size water bottle over it.

TOILET TISSUE

Don't forget it! Nature provides very little to replace this commodity. Try to take only as much of a roll as you will possibly use. Weight conscious packers even go so far as to remove the cardboard center from a small roll. Pack toilet paper where it will be both handy and dry.

TOOTHBRUSH

Travel toothbrushes are nice because the container keeps the bristles straight and clean. One may be found at your dentist's office. Ask him, he will likely give you one. A regular toothbrush can be packed, and kept clean by wrapping the head with plastic wrap or aluminum foil. Toothpaste is left off the list intentionally, in an effort to save weight. Try using salt or baking soda for the short duration of your trip, or at most a sample-size tube of toothpaste.

COMB

Simple, take a pocket comb. Leave brushes at home. They are too bulky for serious backpackers. But, if you are not that serious, go ahead, take a brush. Some women would rather make sacrifices on other equipment, such as fishing tackle.

INSECT REPELLENT

There are many good mosquito repellents on the market. The choice you need to make is how you like to apply it. Lotions, sprays, and towelettes are the most common dispensing methods. Aerosol sprays are the easiest to use, and allow you to *bug proof* clothes as well as skin. Lotions and towelettes are more controllable for protecting delicate facial areas, and are more compact to carry. Depending on the time of year or the climate, you may not even need any. Find out, but if there is any doubt, be sure to include bug dope on your checklist.

Bradley swears cigars are the best repellent. "Light one up and them suckers are gone." It does a pretty fair job of vacating the area of other life forms as well.

PENCIL and NOTE CARDS

A small pencil and a few 3 X 5 note cards are recommended when traveling in groups, or if some of the party is hiking ahead. Leaving notes may be your only form of communication when you don't see others but know your paths will cross. Notes are especially useful when left at camp, indicating where someone has gone, and when they expect to return.

Use a pencil instead of a pen. Pens may leak, go dry, or freeze. Cut the pencil to just two or three inches in length and sharpen. Then you will have the minimum weight, and still have enough length to re-sharpen if necessary. Your pencil can also double as a spool for a small amount of masking tape.

Sturdy note cards are best since they stay in place and remain readable even after a rain shower. You can use regular paper instead of note cards, but be particular where you place memos. A clothespin may prove handy for posting notes.

EXTRA SOCKS

In general, extra clothes are not taken on backpacking excursions. Their bulk and extra pounds often prove to be too much. Socks are the exception to this rule. Feet frequently get damp either from outside moisture or sweating, and footwear needs to be changed to prevent blisters and provide warmth. Pamper your feet. They are the only means of travel you have. Pack whatever kind of stockings you are comfortable wearing, but remember, thick socks with good elasticity are best.

Invest in a couple of pairs of quality hiking socks.

TENNIS SHOES OR MOCCASINS

A change of shoes is almost as important as a change of socks. Boots worn for hiking seem hot and heavy once camp is reached. Changing into light, soft tennis shoes or moccasins feels heavenly to your feet, and lifts your spirits. Some backpackers are tempted to not take a change of shoes in order to save weight. This could be a critical mistake that might make the entire trip miserable. Boots often become wet, so you need something else to wear while they dry.

More than one hiker has discovered that his boots are not sufficiently broken in, and cause excessive blisters. Tennis shoes are not recommended for hiking, but would be a welcome relief from poor fitting or disabled boots. For this reason tennis shoes are preferred over moccasins. Slip-on moccasins are very difficult to hike in, should your boots become unusable.

Another good choice are sandals, which can be used when crossing streams.

PONCHO

Most areas traveled by backpackers have frequent hail or rain showers. Since we normally don't pack a change of clothes, it is crucial to stay dry. Should you get wet, there is a very real danger of hypothermia. You probably won't want to be confined to your shelter whenever it rains, so bring along some rain gear.

A lightweight poncho is a good choice. One that covers only the upper body is acceptable around camp. Should much rain be encountered while hiking, be sure your pack is kept dry as well as yourself. This may require a backpacking poncho that is extra large in the back to cover both hiker and pack. This type of poncho is really only needed if heavy rain is anticipated.

An inexpensive alternative to a poncho is a large plastic garbage bag. Simply cut holes for your head and arms in the bottom of it, and slip it over your shoulders. You'll still need a brimmed hat to complete this arrangement. Don't plan on a garbage bag poncho lasting more than a couple days of use, as they snag and rip very easily. A garbage bag can also make a suitable cover for your sleeping bag.

PLATE, FORK, SPOON and CUP

Utensils and dishes can be packed in a variety of ways. Usually, what you have around the house will do nicely, but don't take mom's best table setting.

For the plate and cup, many campers choose mess kits. These contain a small pot, pan, plate and cup in one nested unit. Mess kits are fine, but there are easier pans to cook with and clean (see Pot, Pan and Spatula).

Sturdy paper plates are the choice of this author. If you are only going for a few days, enough paper plates weigh no more than a single metal one. With paper products there is also the luxury of not having to wash them. Simply chuck them in the campfire.

A spoon and fork can be scavenged from the kitchen, or special backpacking sets can be bought. Stay away from plastic ones, as you need these utensils for cooking and food preparation, as well as eating. If your table fare requires a knife, use the pocketknife you brought along for general use.

A cup is handy for drinking from springs, or serving hot drinks. If big enough, it can double as a small bowl. The cup should have a handle if you are putting anything hot into it. The famous Sierra cup is popular because its handle hooks to a belt or pack, and is readily available while hiking. If you're stealing a cup from home, look for a measuring cup. These usually have handles, and the measurements are useful too.

MEDICATIONS

Double check any medications you may require. A trip could be ruined without them. It's a good idea to pack some pain relievers, as sore muscles are common among backpackers. Antacid tablets are another wise choice for soothing various forms of stomach discomfort.

GROUP ITEMS:

The next category of equipment includes items that could be shared between two or more people. Sharing gear and food saves weight and money, and becomes more of an advantage as a trip gets longer. A disadvantage may be that you have to give others equal privileges to a shared item. Be sure you are compatible with anyone you are sharing with, and that each of you understands how the gear is to be used. Even if you decide not to share any of the following items, you still need to pack them. Don't plan on imposing on someone else who is smart enough to bring them.

TENT or TARP

Backpacking tents come in dozens of designs, sizes, colors, and prices. A whole chapter could easily be written about choosing your "dome away from home." Rather than doing so, let's just give a few pointers on what to look for when purchasing a tent. First, determine what size is needed. Most popular are the two man tents, but lightweight tents are also available for one, three, or four.

The fabric should be rip-stop nylon or something similar if you expect it to last very many trips. If you only want to use it a few times, a less expensive (cheaper) material may be used. A rain fly is a vital feature, since it allows the tent to breathe, eliminating condensation inside while keeping rain out. With a rain fly, a person inside the tent doesn't have to worry about rubbing against the tent walls and "drawing" outside moisture through the wall.

As for design, pick what appeals to you with regards to comfort, pack weight, entry, and ease in erecting. "No trace" campers will suggest that a tent's color should blend into the surroundings. Something in a shade of green or brown is dandy if you don't want to stand out.

Tents are not the only practical means of protection. Tarps can be manipulated in a variety of ways to build warm, dry shelters. Lean-tos and tarp tents can be built with nothing more than a tarp and some rope, providing there are a couple of trees to tie to. Remember, these structures do not have a built-in floor, and can let wind and critters through the open sides. For these reasons they are not suitable for cold weather, but are very comfortable during the summer season.

Bradley doesn't recommend a lean-to in the desert or anywhere else where snakes or scorpions may wish to share your bedroll. Bradley *hates* snakes. But he knows a good joke about a snake bite. Maybe he can tell it to you around the campfire one night, since I don't think it's suitable for publication.

The least costly and lightest shelter is a tent fashioned from a heavy-duty, plastic drop cloth. The cost is minimal, and it weighs only a few ounces. Drop cloths are normally used to cover furniture in storage, but make a fine temporary shield from the elements. To construct a tent, simply run a cord between two trees and drape the drop cloth over it. Pull the edges out to form an A-shaped tent, and place several large smooth rocks to hold the drop cloth to the ground. This material rips easily in a stiff wind so don't plan on this structure lasting more than a couple days, or in rough weather.

ROPE

A short length of rope is a handy, and often necessary piece of tackle. It can be used and re-used for constructing shelters, tying items to a pack, a clothesline, a fish stringer, hanging a food bag, emergency repairs, and a variety of camp projects.

Nylon cord is superior to rope for backpacking purposes. Cord advantages are: it costs less, is more compact, and weighs less than an equivalent length of rope. Nylon, or parachute cord as it is sometimes called, has plenty of strength for normal backpacking needs.

MAP

A single map can accommodate several people hiking together, but never allow hikers to become separated without a map. No matter how much a map is studied before a hike, there will be occasions when the map needs to be referenced.

Topographical maps are the best choice. They illustrate where landmarks and trails are, as well as the steepness of the terrain. Topo maps are a very workable tool with a compass. These maps can be found at a U.S. Geological Survey office. If no such office exists in your town, contact the U.S. Forest Service or your state's Fish and Game Department. Either agency should be able to direct you to a map source for any particular wilderness area you are interested in. Many maps can also be found on the Internet.

If you are looking for a truly inexpensive map, then find the map you need, and photocopy it. A library may contain everything you need.

Protect your map. Lamination is great, but pricey. Try slipping your map inside a sealable plastic pouch, displaying the area you are hiking.

FIRST-AID SUPPLIES

Don't go overboard on first-aid supplies. A few select bandages for cuts and blisters, a tiny tube of antiseptic, and some burn ointment may do for small trips. Large bandages can be fashioned from clothing, a bandanna, or the footless shank of an old athletic sock. Knowing first-aid techniques is your most valuable asset.

Excellent first-aid kits can be bought, but most backpackers find the items they need around the house. Decide what your needs might be, and pack whatever you feel comfortable with. Find out if there are poisonous snakes in the area. If there are none, don't carry the extra weight of a snake bite kit.

NEEDLE

A large needle is your sewing and repair kit. If you have monofilament line packed with your fishing tackle, it can be used in place of thread. The need may arise to mend pants, shoes, or tents, and a single needle is well worth remembering. The needle may be kept with the first aid supplies, and also used for removing slivers and ticks, and heaven forbid, stitching a bad cut. Some hotels furnish a complimentary sewing kit that is the size and shape of a matchbook, so keep your eyes open during your travels.

POT, PAN AND SPATULA

An aluminum pot with handles and a lid is a necessity for preparing most menus. A handle is needed to retrieve the pot from the fire, and a lid keeps ashes and bugs out. Most meals for backpackers require hot water or cooking in a pot.

A frying pan may not be a necessity, but it certainly affords more varied and tasty table fair. It is hard to beat bacon, eggs, flapjacks, or fried fish when feasting in the mountains. The pan should be big enough for the number of people it will be used to cook for. Aluminum is the number one choice of metals for a lightweight fry pan, with an inside coating for easy cleaning. If a campfire is the heat source, you probably won't want to use a nice pan from the kitchen because it's bottom will get black. To keep blackened pots from soiling your pack, stow them in large plastic bags. Coating the outside of the pan with soap limits the amount of blackening.

A small spatula is needed for preparing meals. Its shape allows it to be a mixer, stirring spoon, and food-flipper. If your pot or pan is lined with a non-stick material, then the spatula should not be metal, to avoid scratching the surface.

Mess kits are favorites of some. They provide a small pot, pan, plate, and cup for a single camper, and are compact. A mess kit may be the answer if no one else needs to share the cookware, and you are willing to use a lot of elbow-grease when washing dishes.

STOVE

Today many wilderness areas discourage campfires. At the same time, increasing numbers of backpackers prefer to cook on a small portable stove instead of coals. There are several valid reasons to consider a stove. First, they start easily, even when the woods are soaked by rain. Second, they allow faster, cleaner cooking than does a wood fire, and there is less chance of scorching yourself. Another plus is the ease of dishwashing. Fires blacken pots and pans, making them very difficult to clean.

The only disadvantages of a portable stove are weight and expense, but these must be seriously considered. The butane or propane varieties may weigh a couple of pounds (counting fuel), and take up valuable space inside the pack. Since this is an optional item, if you are on a tight budget, your money might be better spent on something else. You'll want to decide whether or not a burner is worth taking on your next excursion.

FOOD

Food is only mentioned here because it is a possible group item. It will be discussed in detail in a later chapter, but note that sharing menus saves weight, money and time, and allows the chores associated with meal preparation and clean up to be split between campers.

SALT and PEPPER

Even if menus are not shared it may be okay to share such amenities as salt and pepper. Since the taste of many dishes depend on salt, it is a good idea to list it separately on your packing list. Salt and pepper can be packed in individual serving size, so pick up a few extra at the next fast food joint you visit. With individual packets you can pack exactly what is needed for each meal, plus a few extra for miscalculations. Packets also prevent spillage inside your pack. Oh, and keep the S&P dry. Wet salt is the pits.

SCOUR PAD

A scouring pad compatible with cooking surfaces will clean pots and pans. Do not use pads containing soap, unless you plan on washing and rinsing all dishes away from lakes and streams. Try elbow-grease instead. A good scouring pad is all that is needed to wash all of the dishes. One easy method is to warm some water in the pot used for cooking, and use it for a dish washing basin.

OPTIONAL ITEMS:

The following list of items can be classified as optional. They are not necessary for survival or comfort, but may be for fun. These are either lightweight luxury items, or gear for pursuing a favorite hobby or pastime. When adding optional items to your pack there are two rules to follow. The first is K.I.S.S. (keep it simple, stupid), and the second is to remember that you have to carry it, on your back, for many miles. These basic rules might be overlooked by zealous hikers, but if you do, you may be sorry after a few hours on the trail.

FISHING GEAR

Since fishing ranks high as a reason to go backpacking, it becomes important to pack the necessary tackle. Again the key word is *necessary*. If you can, determine exactly the type of fishing you will be doing, and pack only enough gear to get you through the trip. You don't need the whole tackle box! Many anglers take along extra rod, reel, and line. Despite the extra weight, this is an excellent choice for avid fishermen. It would be heartbreaking to pack into some fantastic fishing, only to have your fishing gear break with no available replacement.

For ease in packing, put all leaders, hooks, sinkers, lures, flies, and bubbles into one container. A small single level tackle box, an empty kitchen match box, or a sealable plastic bag will suffice.

Artificial lures are usually your best bet, especially for high country trout. Bait is quite heavy in comparison, and should only be needed if you are uncomfortable using lures or flies, or if scouting reports indicate the fish really are biting bait best. A call to your local Fish and Game Department or tackle store may help.

CAMERA

Amateur and professional photographers alike should have a field day on any backpacking excursion. Depending on how important photography is to you will probably determine how much and what kind of equipment to take.

If the camera uses batteries, make sure they are fresh, or take extra along. You can use most any camera, but there are some nice cameras especially designed for backpackers and skiers that fit into a shirt pocket. Pack the camera in a place where it is readily accessible, such as a pack side pocket or a belt pouch. There will be plenty of wonderful opportunities for shutterbugs all along the trail.

SAW

A saw shouldn't be needed for cutting firewood. This chore can be accomplished with large rocks thrown against thinner logs, but watch out for flying sticks. If logs can't be broken using this method, they are either too thick or too green to burn. However, a saw may be a useful tool for constructing primitive shelters where permitted. Good saws for backpackers are folding or string saws. Folding saws are much quicker than string saws, which are lighter and less expensive. If a saw is really necessary, the folding variety is highly recommended.

PLIERS

A small pair of needle nose pliers is one of the handiest tools you can bring. They have many practical uses around camp, ranging from retrieving a hot pan from the fire to dislodging fish hooks from unfortunate fishermen. Find a pair with a wire cutter inset, and have another tool for no extra weight.

SPADE

Large groups should opt to carry along a garden spade or small hand shovel. Its main purpose is to dig a suitable latrine for everyone. Small parties can usually get by without one if they exercise care.

Do not use a spade, or anything else, to dig drainage trenches around tents. This practice scars our precious wilderness for years to come. Pitch tents in a spot not threatened by water runoff.

SAFETY PIN

A large safety pin can be included as part of a sewing or repair kit. You'll be glad you brought it if you need to make a quick repair to clothing. Pants that split out, snaps that break, and buttons that pop off can be repaired by a common safety pin. It can also be fashioned into a fish hook in a survival situation.

Bradley likes to pin his damp socks to the outside of his pack while hiking, permitting them to dry. This is a great idea, but I always make sure I'm upwind from Bradley when he's practicing this technique.

WATCH

One of the niceties of backpacking is that you don't have to watch the clock. However, a wrist or pocket watch becomes a necessity if your group will be splitting up temporarily, either on the trail or exploring around camp. You may have a definite need to know when to meet someone, or know when another group should be returning from a side trip. The time of day can be deceptive in the mountains. With a watch, one can calculate if he has enough time for a jaunt away from camp, and still be able to make it back before dark.

A watch can help you estimate how far you've traveled. Most backpackers average 1.5 to 2 miles per hour.

SUNGLASSES

If you expect to spend considerable time fishing or in the sun, then a good pair of polarized sunglasses are recommended. Severe eye strain is no laughing matter, and can be avoided by donning some shades on bright days, or when facing reflective waters. Sunglasses are required gear when traversing large snow fields. Be careful to pack them where they won't be crushed by shifting equipment.

MIRROR

A miniature handle-less mirror serves dual purposes. People still like to spruce up and comb their hair, even when roughing it. A single pocket size mirror can easily be used by several campers.

The second use of a mirror is signaling. Signal mirrors are shatter-proof, have a hole in the middle, and are fairly inexpensive. Should you become lost, a flashing mirror can be seen by searchers for miles. You may wish to practice this method of communicating among your group during backcountry activities.

WHISTLE

An emergency whistle becomes a valuable instrument should you get lost or injured. Blowing on a whistle expends little energy, and can be heard for long distances. Kids should *always* carry one in their pocket.

HAND SOAP

If your backpacking trip lasts longer than overnight, or if fish will be handled, then soap is certainly appropriate. Pack a small tube or bar. Either a hotel sample or a bar shrunken from use will do. Never use soap in any water source, even if the soap is biodegradable. Sporting goods stores stock biodegradable liquid hand soap among the backpacking accessories.

"Keeping clean keeps the flies and mosquitoes away, while keeping dirty keeps people away." These are more words of wisdom from Bradley. My question is: How do I keep bugs and people away?

SUN PROTECTION CREAM

Very few of us are used to being in the outdoors all day long. Those with fair skin may need some help avoiding sunburn to delicate areas such as the nose, neck, ears, and arms. Some hikers prefer short pants, and will need skin protection for their legs unless they sport a great tan. If you are hoping to improve your tan, then use suntan lotion.

Many outdoorsmen use sunblock lotion to keep from burning during long days of exposure. Sunrays are more damaging as altitude increases. Also, burning rays come not only from the sun above, but from reflective lakes, streams, and snow fields. Keep adequately covered with a long sleeve collared shirt, long trousers, and a brimmed hat.

LIP-BALM

One of the first signs of dehydration is chapped lips. A chap-stick can curtail mild chapping, or bring welcome relief to dry lips. Lip-balm also comes in sunblock formulas for people that have sensitive lips that easily burn. An added advantage of a sunblock formula is that you can also apply it your skin. Put it on high profile areas such as your nose, cheeks, ears, and neck.

SALT TABLETS

Strenuous hiking sweats away valuable salts and minerals that need replacing to avoid fatigue. Salt tablets are excellent for restoring body salts. These supplements can be picked up at any pharmacy without a prescription. Be sure you understand how much to take, and how often to take them. If instructions are lacking on the container, consult your pharmacist or doctor. Generally, if you have been hiking for a couple of hours and sweating, then one tablet every two to four hours while hiking will replace what your body is losing through perspiration.

Snacks high in salt content can be eaten to replenish lost body salts. Salted peanuts are excellent since they provide quick energy as well. Whether taking salt tablets or salty snacks, drink extra water to prevent dehydration. As much as a quart of water between salt tablets is suggested.

If you choose to use salt tablets, look for ones that also contain potassium chloride (KCL). These will help reduce the risk of heart attack by replacing potassium lost through body fluids.

BANDANNA

Another optional but highly useful item is the bandanna. It can be used for: wiping off dirt and sweat, a hand towel, a handkerchief, an emergency bandage or sling, or a hot pad. If the air becomes dusty, as it can on a dry trail, then make like a cowboy and secure the bandanna around your mouth and nose for easier breathing.

A clean bandanna can be used as a filter when filling your canteen. This doesn't make the water safe to drink, only cleaner. If the water source has small bits of debris floating through it, simply stretch your bandanna across the canteen's opening, and the bandanna will screen out any noticeable particles. Bradley claims he gets a salty flavor in his water whenever he attempts bandanna-screening. Hmmm.

WATER PURIFICATION (TABLETS or PUMP?)

Iodine tablets have been used for many years to sterilize water, but you had better follow directions closely. If the directions say to wait thirty minutes after adding the tablets, then wait! Anything less and giardia may still be lurking.

Purification pumps are popular these days if you can afford the price and the weight. They are also a lot of work to get a little water; but if you're hiking an area with questionable water, then a pump may prove to be your safest bet. This is a tough choice to make, especially when the budget is tight. I have often done just fine searching for springs, or boiling my water.

GLOVES

A pair of work gloves are great hand savers. They provide protection while gathering wood or handling hot pans, and feel real good when the temperature plunges.

CANDLE

A candle is a great fire starter when kindling is damp, or a pesky breeze makes lighting tough.

PLAYING CARDS

Bad weather is common in the wilderness, and may confine you to quarters for a long period of time. The time will seem shorter if you can pass it playing cards. A regular deck will do, but there are other options. Miniature decks are available, or there are informational playing cards with survival or camping tips on them.

Other enjoyable alternatives might be compact travel-size games such as checkers or chess.

BOOK or JOURNAL

Another time killer or relaxant is a good book. Keep it light by choosing a slim paperback. You probably won't have a lot of time to read anyway, unless it is your selected activity.

A journal can be as simple as a nineteen-cent notepad, or as nice as a leather bound notebook designed especially for the task.

Just as photographs remind us of the sights of a trip, a journal can be used to recall the fine details that turn a trip into an adventure. Describe not only the sights, but the sounds, smells, tastes, and feelings (physical and emotional). There is no better time than the present to record your thoughts, especially when the present is in the backcountry.

DAY PACK

If extended hikes away from camp are planned, a small day pack is desirable. You may wish to tote a camera, fishing gear, canteen, jacket, poncho, and snacks with you on side trips. Small nylon shoulder or fanny packs are fine choices. You can avoid bringing a day pack if your clothing has several large pockets, and you don't mind awkward bulges.

Whew, that's quite a list of backpacking equipment. Thanks for bearing with me through this lengthy but necessary chapter. Hopefully, now you can tailor gear to comfortably fit your pack and pocketbook. Clothing you might pack, such as a jacket, will be discussed later, as will food. You can take anything else you want, but remember, you have to carry it!

4

What Not to Take

If you thought of something to include in your pack, but it was not on the list of recommended gear, then think again. Chances are, the item is on the list of equipment to leave behind. What you don't take is almost as important as what you do. Heavy loads can and must be avoided. Some outdoor gear simply has no practical use in primitive wilderness, or perhaps it might risk someone's safety, and is better off left behind with the roadside campers.

All of the items mentioned in this chapter have been found in the packs of novices, as well as some not-so-novice packers. Try not to laugh. Usually, the unnecessary gear was noticed after camp was reached, while the guilty person complained of a sore back or shoulders. You can steer clear of these mistakes by understanding why certain equipment is undesirable.

HATCHET

Several extra pounds are added to your load if a hatchet is thrown in. Hatchets are commonly used to chop firewood. In the backcountry, bonfires are discouraged, so large logs are not needed. As a general rule, any log that can't be broken with a large rock (say 25 pounds), is either too thick or too green for the type of fire you should be building.

Don't take a hatchet with thoughts of chopping into live trees. The backwoods are much too fragile to allow destruction to any living thing. Most wilderness areas enforce regulations against harvesting or damaging live trees.

SHOVEL

The only digging you should be doing is scooping out a cat hole latrine. A shovel could do this with ease, but the weight of even a small collapsible shovel makes it prohibitive to carry. A garden spade as described in the previous chapter will take a little longer to do the job, but is light enough and small enough to pack.

SHEATH KNIFE

For safety reasons, sheath knives should be left at home and saved for hunting season. Once unsheathed, these knives can easily cause an accident even when not in use, and that's what makes them undesirable to backpackers. Every safety precaution must be taken to avoid any serious injury in remote wilderness, where medical assistance is miles away by foot. Take along a knife with a folding blade. They are much safer than the sheath variety, and are available in any popular size.

CANNED FOOD

Food in a can has several disadvantages. The first is weight. A large percentage of the weight is water, which is easily added to dried foods at camp. If you were to pack canned food, you would also need to bring a can opener, adding more extra ounces. The can itself is an inconvenience. Besides its additional weight, it must be packed out after use. Never attempt to bury or burn tin cans, as they will not decompose and may be uncovered by animals. Any food or drink in glass containers should be shunned for all the same reasons, plus the possibility of shattering.

RAW FRUITS & VEGETABLES

As good as raw fruits and vegetables are, they need to be forgotten. Water weight is the sole enemy. You still should plan fruits and vegies into your diet, but make sure they are dehydrated or dried. Supermarkets provide a wide selection of dried fruits and trail mix if you choose to buy. For the do-it-yourselfer, try drying sliced produce in a dehydrator, or in an oven set on low with the door propped open a few inches.

CAST IRON SKILLET

A Yosemite Park ranger was once asked, "what was the most common mistake by backcountry travelers." He said he was amazed at the number of people who had cast iron skillets protruding from their packs. While it's true that you probably need a frying pan, cast iron is out of the question. It is many times heavier than its aluminum counterpart, and is more difficult to clean. On that long uphill climb, when ounces turn to pounds, cast iron must feel like a ton of bricks.

EXTRA CLOTHES

A change of clothes is a heavy luxury most backpackers can do without. Pants are especially bulky, and should only be packed if you are going on a lengthy trip, or if you prefer hiking in shorts. It is more common to not pack extra trousers.

You'll need an extra pair of socks and a thick, warm shirt to change into after the hike, but that's about the extent of extra clothes. You will most likely pack other articles of clothing such as a jacket, poncho, and hat, but these are not duplicates of anything you are already wearing. In summary, avoid packing two of anything except socks and a shirt, including what you wear.

Bradley says he likes to take an extra T-shirt so he has a fresh shirt to wear on the hike out. I once witnessed Bradley make a pass at a great looking gal after spending four days in the high country. She was obviously *not* impressed with his fresh T-shirt. But he still packs one.

PILLOW

It may seem silly, but this author has witnessed neophytes pack a large fluffy pillow fifteen miles. I am sure the pillow was enjoyed much more at camp than it was on the trail. Pillows take up too much space in the pack, not to mention a few pounds of weight, to ever be seriously considered as a necessity. Most backpackers will wad up an article of clothing such as a jacket, to use as a pillow. This technique is plenty adequate for any wilderness experience. Some sleeping bag duffels can be converted into pillows. If the wadded jacket technique is not sufficient for your needs, backpacking pillows can be bought for under five bucks. These "pillows" are just flannel lined bags that can be stuffed with dry clothing.

PAJAMAS

To some, pajamas may not sound that far fetched, but remember, you're supposed to be roughing it. Unless you absolutely cannot sleep without them, try it without. Women may need pajamas for extra warmth, as they generally have a lower body metabolism to keep them warm through the night, and they have more of a problem when nature calls than do men.

FLOTATION DEVICES

Any item designed to keep you afloat should be shunned for safety and weight reasons. These devices include such things as inflatable rafts, stout air mattresses, life jackets, and float tubes. Besides flotation devices being extremely cumbersome, it is safer to stay off icy wilderness waters. Once again, safety first. If you really want to try rubber rafts, then use horses to carry your gear.

TOWEL

You probably will want to wash up each day, but a towel won't be needed. Bathing and swimming will usually be out of the question, and you should be able to air dry from hand washing. A towel is one of the comforts of home that needs to remain there, but then most backpackers enjoy getting by with minimal provisions for a short period of time. Remember, your bandanna can be used for a temporary hand towel.

TOOTHPASTE

Save every ounce you can! Instead of toothpaste, try using baking soda or salt for the duration of the trip. Chances are you already have enough stocked with the food. A little dental floss is nice, since its weight is negligible.

SHAVING NEEDS

Let your whiskers grow. The shaving cream and razor can wait until your return. If you positively cannot stand the itch stubble inflicts, bring a razor but not the shaving cream. To soften whiskers, enough lather can be worked up using hand soap. The same reasoning can be applied to the hair on a woman's legs.

Oh, and be sure to shave just before leaving home.

HAIR BRUSH

Well maybe a woman with long or thick hair will want a hair brush, but for everyone else it is too heavy for the job. You won't be in a beauty contest, so work it out with a pocket comb.

MAKEUP

Women, if you can't go natural for a few days, then perhaps you might be happier with another outdoor activity. Believe me, the men won't mind at all, seeing you without makeup. And if any of you guys are using makeup, knock it off!

MUSIC PLAYER

You go backpacking to "get away from it all." Don't pollute yours or anyone else's wilderness experience by bringing along a radio, CD player, iPod, etcetera. There are plenty of pleasing sounds in the backwoods, if you only listen.

If you are still not convinced to forget the music, consider its added weight. Still dying for a music fix? Take headphones. Just don't let me hear it!

GASOLINE

Flammable liquids to aid fire starting are dangerous and unnecessary. Gas could spill in your pack, ruining gear and food, or could explode under certain conditions. Anything that jeopardizes safety or equipment must be discouraged. You'll be hours away from help should an accident occur.

GUNS

Unless hunting is a planned activity, leave all firearms behind. Guns are just another accident waiting to happen in a world where you cannot afford one. Also, they present an extremely heavy load. One possible exception to tote a gun would be if you are hiking in country where you are likely to encounter bears. However, many of these areas prohibit firearms, and bear spray is more effective.

If you should pack a gun, know the local hunting seasons, laws, and restrictions. Above all, be extra, extra careful.

This chapter suggests many items not to pack. Each item has made this classification for one or more of the following reasons:

- Too heavy
- Not safe
- Not necessary
- Destructive
- Something else may be substituted.

If you are considering taking an item that was not mentioned as something you should or should not take, just review the five reasons listed above. Then decide if you still want to carry it for the entire duration of your backpacking adventure.

5

Pig Out

Eating in the great outdoors is more than just a necessary routine. A camper's senses of taste and smell are greatly enhanced. The aesthetic surroundings coupled with increased activity hones all senses and builds huge appetites. Dining in the wilderness can be extremely pleasurable, while at the same time providing one's body with the nutrients needed to keep up with the strenuous demands of backpacking. This is not the time to go on a diet. Eat up! Mega-calories are absolutely essential to keep energy levels high.

Although special considerations must be made when deciding what foods to take, you can prepare a delicious menu with plenty of variety throughout any trip. First, let's rule out items we must avoid to keep pack weight feasible. Any food or drink in a can is out; bottles too. Water weight must not be carried. It can be added at meal time. Raw fruits and vegetables should be shunned for the same reason. Frozen foods, fresh dairy products, and bakery goodies all perish too quickly, even if their weight wasn't prohibitive. It may seem like we have ruled out the entire supermarket, and will have to resort to tasteless, expensive, dehydrated packets. Not so.

Most dehydrated foods are a bit bland at best, and can easily cost upwards of seven dollars per meal. In this chapter you will hopefully discover a wide array of tasty healthy menus that can be economically purchased at a grocery store, or easily made at home. Eating on the trail can cost less than eating at home, and can satisfy even the most particular palate. Perhaps it's only your increased appetite, but outdoor meals can be satisfying and easy, if planned properly.

As with most aspects of backpacking, planning is the crucial phase. The menu prepared before an excursion is equivalent in importance to having a checklist for gear. What you eat largely determines how you feel, and how much you enjoy your backcountry experience. Don't skip planning, and risk feeling poorly.

Another big advantage of meal planning is weight control. No, not your weight, the pack's. With good planning, you can pack sufficient food at the rate of one pound per day. Even lengthy trips are possible without bulky, unbearable pack loads.

When deciding on menus, it is important to consider the type of activities you expect to do after eating. The food should complement what you do following the meal, or early the next day. For example, don't eat a heavy breakfast just before a strenuous hike, but dine on a big dinner the evening before to store some energy. This is true not only for the hike in, but for long day hikes, and the trek back to civilization.

Expected weather may give you a clue of what food to pack. If cold weather is in the forecast, be sure to include plenty of hot drinks and maybe some packaged soups. Extremely hot climates may dictate packing extra rations of cool drink mixes and salty foods.

Fancy recipes are not mandatory to enjoy tasty meals. If you prefer to cook exotic meals, that's great, but most outdoorsmen would rather prepare their grub quick and easy. For that reason, the following chapter will not attempt to describe detailed recipes, but should enlighten you enough to be able to plan fulfilling menus tailored around your activities.

When planning menus, start with dinner the day before beginning your hike. Plan a big meal of pasta, noodles, potatoes, or beans; and include lots of bread. These foods are loaded with complex carbohydrates, which are stored as much needed energy for the following day's trek. A person that eats a spaghetti or lasagna supper will have significantly more stamina the next day than someone having a big steak. Items in the carbohydrate category should be planned the day before any hard physical exertion. Other excellent carbohydrate sources are whole grain cereals (oatmeal), and nuts.

Quick energy is the next food related benefit your body requires. Although some sugars are in regular meals, the majority of instant energy comes from snacks. Grocery stores are teaming with wonderful snacks that give you the quick boost needed to outlast a steep mountain trail. Don't pack any chocolate. It will probably cause a mess when it melts. Nuts are great suppliers of energy, and if salted, may replace some body salt lost through perspiration. Be sure to drink plenty of water with salty snacks to prevent dehydration.

Trail mix or granola bars are other handy treats that give a quick lift. Trail mix can be bought or can be blended at home using your own preferred mixture of candy, nuts, and dried fruits.

Certain meal time foods provide quick energy too. If you think you will need fast energy right after a meal, then work some pudding, dried fruit, jam, syrup, or marshmallows into the menu. Pre-sweetened punch can also assist your energy needs.

Dried fruits offer natural sugars that are superb sources of instant energy. Raisins are delicious, and can be bought in convenient package sizes. You can also buy other dried fruits, but many hikers prefer to dry fruit such as apples, apricots, bananas, and cherries at home. Drying at home can be performed with a food dryer, oven, or even the sun if the fruit is properly protected from insects. Whatever fruit you choose, you can be assured of an excellent source of natural sugar.

Now is probably a good time to explain the difference between dried and dehydrated. Dried means having most of the moisture evaporated out, leaving the fruit chewy. Dehydrated foods have all the water extracted out, and are hard and inedible until water is added back.

Another important benefit of fruit is maintaining regularity. All of the physical exertion and sweating of backpacking tends to dehydrate a body, which causes constipation. Drink lots of fluids, and always plan some fruit into menus to be assured your bowels keep functioning normally. Foods with roughage also help digestion. High fiber cereals and popcorn are good choices to aid regularity. Oatmeal, although not the tastiest, is one of the healthiest ways to start off a day. Later on, popcorn pops into a satisfying afternoon or evening treat.

During long hikes, your body sweats away valuable salts and minerals that need to be replaced. Salty snacks are helpful and supply calories too. Favorites for backpackers include nuts, crackers, chips, popcorn, jerky, and soup made from bouillon cubes. Be sure to replace lost body salts one way or the other, or you'll probably be too fatigued to fully enjoy your backwoods experience.

Potassium also needs replacing. Bananas are well known as a provider of potassium, but there are other much more potent sources. The best feasible potassium suppliers include dried apricots, peaches, dates, raisins, peanuts, walnuts, and molasses.

Although it is not essential to maintain a balanced diet for the short duration of a backpacking trip, doing so will assure better performance. Proteins give balance to menus, and provide long lasting energy, strength, resistance, and stamina. Traditional protein sources are eggs, bacon, nuts, peanut butter, beans, bread, jerky, and fish. If fresh fish are planned for a meal, it would be wise to pack a substitute dish in case they're not biting. Alpine trout are notorious for hitting all day long until you decide to catch dinner, then they disappear.

Vitamin tablets are an efficient means of supplying daily requirements for the duration of a wilderness trek. Since raw or canned vegetables are shunned because of water weight, it is a good idea to provide this missing link in tablet form. Resume a balanced diet, including fresh greens, upon returning home.

Now that we have discussed the basic food requirements and what types of food can be planned into your menus, you may like to see some sample menus. But, before doing that, lets review some handy tips on preparing and packing meals. Much time, weight, work, and grief can be saved by using a few simple ideas. Probably the most important rule for serious backpackers to adhere to is "only pack exactly what is needed". This requires precise planning and repackaging, but is worth the effort in pounds saved.

After determining what the menus are for each meal, figure out how much of each item is needed. If only half a package is needed, don't carry a whole one. Measure out the necessary amount into a sealable plastic bag. Include any unfamiliar cooking instructions. *Food weight can be reduced by as much as fifty percent* by following this simple procedure.

Pack each meal's contents together to prevent rummaging through the food supply to prepare dinner or breakfast. The exception to this would be foods that must be kept cool. They are best packed together to prolong their cooler temperature. Refrigerate perishables in a snow bank, stream, or lake once camp is reached. This task is an easy one if all meats, eggs, and cheeses are packed together in a water tight container. Sealable plastic storage bags are ideal.

To illustrate how to plan proper meals for backpacking, sample menus have been prepared for a four day, three night trip. Immediately following the ingredients for each meal will be a brief explanation as to why certain foods were selected, and their benefits. Entrees were chosen based on planned activities. In this case we are planning on hiking in the first day, and out the last day. In between, short day hikes and fishing are planned.

Most backpacking trips begin in the cool of the morning, with a light breakfast before hiking. The first meal that needs to be packed is dinner. Only plan on two meals each day. A solid breakfast, and a hefty dinner at about three or four in the afternoon will be enough. If hunger strikes between meals, or extra energy is needed, nibble on snacks.

FIRST DAY - DINNER
    Steak
    Hash-brown potatoes (box)
    Powdered Milk
    Candy

It may seem we have broken the rules already by bringing along a juicy steak, but for the first evening it's

OK. Besides being extremely delicious, a steak provides valuable cell reproducing proteins your body craves after a hard hike. As with any strenuous exercise, muscles are stretched (actually torn slightly), and protein speeds the recovery process. Freeze the steak before packing it, and it should be thawed for cooking by supper time. Plenty of hash-browns round out the meal tastefully, while satisfying big appetites. Potatoes must be of the boxed variety, so all of the water weight is added just before cooking.

Your body's calcium reserves can get seriously depleted on a long hike. Powdered milk is a good source of calcium. Replenishing bodily nutrients is a critical factor for a successful long trek. You need to feel good to have fun.

You have probably noticed we don't have as many courses as you might have at home. The objective is to furnish a simple, satisfying meal. Be sure to bring a large enough quantity of each menu item to fill everyone up. A few bites of candy will supply a quick lift for evening chores, such as gathering firewood or fly casting to some hungry trout.

Second Day - Breakfast
    Bacon
    Eggs
    Hot chocolate
    Dried fruit (your choice)

A bacon and eggs breakfast is the traditional mountain breakfast. It is also my preferred way to please the taste buds and the tummy. Plan on more than you usually eat—actually double. Appetites are increased by the previous day's activities and the wilderness setting. This meal will not digest quickly, keeping the pangs of hunger away until mid-afternoon. Top it off with hot chocolate for a burst of energy to get you moving, and some dried fruit to maintain regularity.

When packing eggs, the larger the eggs the easier they break. Medium eggs seem most efficient, and can be safely hauled in the carton they are purchased in. Larger eggs may crack during rough treatment, leaving you with a mess and no breakfast. As a safeguard, secure the egg carton inside a plastic bag. Some backpackers take no chances, and break their eggs into a sturdy container before packing them.

Second Day - Dinner
    Soup
    Crackers
    Seasoned Noodles
    Beef sticks
    Pudding

Start off with a soup mix of your choice, and crackers. Some soups are miniature balanced meals in themselves, and crackers supply carbohydrates and salt. A couple of hearty beef sticks comprise the meat course, served with a generous helping of seasoned noodles, or rice if you'd rather. There are numerous varieties of noodle, macaroni, and rice dishes available at the supermarket. A dessert of pudding adds the sugar you'll desire. An instant pudding mix is the lightest way to go, but requires preparation. I prefer small pudding cups. Their weight is manageable, and the containers can be burned.

It is important to note that boiling a pot of water takes longer at high altitudes; about two degrees per thousand feet to be exact. To translate that into time, double the cooking time *every* six thousand feet. Choose foods that require little cooking time, otherwise you may have a long wait for a meal. Frying is affected very little by altitude, and is often my preferred method of heating up some grub.

Third Day - Breakfast
    Bacon
    Fresh fish
    Pancakes with jam or molasses
    Hot chocolate

If the fish are going to bite, you should have them figured out by now. Try catching some fresh ones for breakfast, and fry them in bacon grease. A light coating of flour and cornmeal is optional. Either way, fresh fried fish are a sensational morning treat. Even if you can't hook any, there is still enough to eat with this menu. Hot cakes made from a complete mix will fill you up. Jam is suggested instead of syrup because it is less likely to spill in your pack, and is available in individual serving sizes. Collect jams as you patronize restaurants throughout the year, then sample them on pancakes in the high country. Mmmm. Molasses is a good option, as it is an excellent provider of potassium, which may be running low because of your increased activity. Hot chocolate is on the slate again, but you may wish to substitute hot or cold instant orange drink.

Third Day - Dinner
    Casserole with flaked fish
    Beef broth
    Dried fruit

Grocery stores stock several different tuna casserole mixes that are light and easy to prepare. Don't bring the tuna however. Catch a few fish and fry them. Then flake the fish similar to tuna, and use them in the casserole. Noodles are the main ingredient of the meal, and rightfully so. They will provide stored energy to be released while hiking out the next day. If the fish quit biting, at least the noodle portion of the casserole is still available. Always look upon fish as a bonus.

Beef broth derived from bouillon cubes makes a fine supper drink, and replenishes lost body salts. Another suitable drink might be herbal tea, which is nice to have along for relief of unexpected nausea. Dried fruits for dessert leave a sweet taste in your mouth, as well as supplying quick energy and roughage to your diet.

Fourth Day - Breakfast
    Instant oatmeal
    Raisins
    Hot chocolate

This is the last meal of the trip. It should be light and easy to fix. The arduous trek out demands a light digestible breakfast. Instant oatmeal fits these requirements to a tee. Raisins may be added to the oatmeal or eaten plain. Include hot chocolate, and the only preparation needed for breakfast is to boil a pot of water. By this time you will probably be a bit tired, and anxious to pack out, so reward yourself by keeping breakfast as simple as possible.

For more ideas on possible snacks and menu items, check the menu planner (appendix B) in the back of this book. Oh, here's one final backwoods tip to remember: "Camp food tastes better in the dark." Bradley and I will vouch for that.

6

What's a Backpacker to Wear?

Weather conditions in the high country can change dramatically in an hour. Storms come and go quickly, and in some areas are a daily event. Determining what to wear on a backpacking trip can be a critical decision. The clothes you wear plus those in your pack must protect you from all the brutal elements of nature. And *brutal* they can be! Whether it be sudden cold, drenching rain, searing sun, biting insects, thick brush, or poisonous plants, your clothes are your protection.

Clothing should be worn in layers of breathable fabrics. By taking along an undershirt or T-shirt, a long sleeve flannel shirt, a sweater or jacket, a poncho, and a hat, you can add or subtract garments to match any weather you may encounter. You might also want to adjust the amount of clothing you wear to coincide with how active you plan on being. Strenuous activities, like hiking, require less clothing than passive pastimes such as fishing.

This book has not addressed winter camping, and will not start now. Since camping in the snow and freezing temperatures is only attempted by a small brave percentage of campers, we will cover the more popular seasons. Although summer temperatures occasionally dip below freezing, they never come close to the sub-zero readings of winter. Let's begin.

BOOTS

Footwear is the first article of clothing we will cover, and rightfully so. A good pair of boots are the single most important thing you'll wear. They are your sole (pun intended) means of transportation, as you travel open expanses of wilderness. Quality is not to be sacrificed when it comes to hiking boots. This doesn't mean you need the best boots money can buy, but rather that you should double check the condition of your boots. Have no doubt they will serve you throughout the entire trek.

There are two basic styles of boots commonly used for backpacking. Mountaineering boots have been worn for years, but more recently, lightweight hiking boots have gained popularity. A pair of mountaineering boots weigh in at about five pounds. These boots are extremely sturdy, but are generally too much boot for most backpacking. Unless you plan on scaling serious mountain peaks, hiking boots are your best bet.

Hiking boots come in many styles and materials. Some lightweight models are now made by well-known tennis shoe manufacturers. Each have their own advantages and disadvantages. Their weight is about half that of mountaineering boots. This is a tremendous plus considering how many thousands of times you lift your feet during the course of a trip. Find a lightweight pair that best fits you and your wallet.

Lug soles are found on the majority of backpacking footwear. The deep tread prevents slippage on wet trails and steep mountain sides. They also provide solid support for the entire length of the foot. This is especially valuable when crossing rocky terrain. If you have ever attempted a long day hike wearing tennis shoes, you can certainly appreciate the stiffer lug sole.

Gusseted tongues (attached to boot sides) are a must, and all worthy boots will have them. Gusseting keeps water, sand, and pebbles outside the boot where they belong.

Good boots also feature a reinforced toe. The front of boots take a real pounding as they bounce off boulders and tree roots. The more tired your legs become, the less you raise them, and consequently the more rocks your feet will bump. Extra toe support is necessary for downhill trekking, as toes slide forward with each step. As you can see, footwear without lug soles and adequate toe protection can make hiking a miserable feat (oops, another pun).

Shopping for boots may not be a task you enjoy, but how you shop can determine how comfortable you will be on the trail. Before shopping, slip on a pair of extra thick socks, similar to what you wear backpacking. When trying on boots, ask for a half size larger than your normal shoe size. Even with hiking socks on, your toe should have ample space for forward movement. This prevents jamming of toes on those rough downhill slopes. Also, boot length shrinks as boots gradually mold to your feet. Walk around the shoe store until you are confident the boots will be comfortable for your feet. Not all styles are. To avoid blisters, there should be a little slippage, but no hard rub on the heel. The front portion should feel a little spacious. Even though you are wearing thick socks, you still need to allow for your feet to swell slightly. During a long hike, it is normal for feet to expand by as much as half a shoe size.

Budget Alert! Watch the newspaper ads throughout the year, especially during January and February. Stores specializing in backpacking gear often feature name brand hiking boots at less than half the regular price. Why? These boots may be last year's models or "seconds" with minor cosmetic blemishes. But that hardly matters. During your first outing, you'll add several imperfections of your own.

After getting your new boots home, thoroughly break them in before using them on a long hike. Stiff boots can be crippling after several tough miles in the mountains. One excellent way to break in boots is to wear them on short walks. You should be walking anyway to improve muscle tone and lung capacity. Obtain the added benefit of getting your feet and legs accustomed to walking with the weight of hiking boots.

A couple of useful accessories for boots are moleskin and extra shoelaces. Moleskin is a sticky padding that can be applied to the foot on areas susceptible to blisters. They are a superior preventative measure. Duct tape is a fine substitute for moleskin, and is thinner, so it doesn't alter boot fit. Extra shoelaces might come in handy, but you can get by just fine with some nylon cord, which may already be packed for other uses.

CAMP SHOES

Once camp is reached, it feels good to change into camp shoes. Sandals or tennis shoes work great for this purpose. Keep these shoes lightweight, since they will be in your pack during the hike in.

Having a change of footwear has several advantages. Your boots will have a chance to dry or air out. Weary feet feel more comfy, and rejuvenate faster in soft shoes. And finally, look upon camp shoes as your spare tire. If for some unexpected reason your boots become unusable, you still have something to walk in.

SOCKS

Tight socks are a must. This prevents them from bunching up inside your boots. Anytime socks can form a wad, you risk getting a blister at that spot. Stockings with good elasticity extending up the calf are preferred.

Most hikers wear thick socks. Thickness provides an extra comfort cushion, and minimizes boot rub. Include at least one change of socks in your pack, even if just on an overnighter. Socks, just as shoes, need a chance to freshen up and dry out. Some hikers prefer wearing two pair of socks. Thick socks over thin liners prevent blisters, and wick away sweat.

UNDERWEAR

Even if you don't wear an undershirt around home, you may wish to consider doing so on a backpacking trip. It gives you an extra layer of clothing in case the weather turns foul. Choose a breathable fabric such as cotton, or fish net. Avoid hot, clammy nylon. Some hikers pack extra undergarments. This is a good idea on lengthy trips, or if you expect to get soaked at a river crossing.

PANTS

Loose pants are recommended. Tight pants restrict movement, and legs have to work harder with each step. Legs have enough work to do without fighting the pull of snug pants.

The best material for trousers is cotton. Denim is not as good, as it tends to chafe skin when wet, and takes a long time to dry. Backpacking pants should not be as long as slacks you wear around home. If too long, the bottoms tend to become soaked easily when passing through wet meadows or trails. Cuffs are also a problem. They are notorious collectors of dirt and pine needles, so find a pair without cuffs.

Hiking shorts are worn by many nature lovers. These are fine in warm climates, but always pack a pair of long pants for when the mercury drops or the sun burns. If long pants are worn, carrying shorts is optional. The reverse is not true. You always need long trousers along.

Shorts also prove to be a distinct disadvantage in mosquito country, or where there is thick brush or poisonous plants. If you really prefer hiking in shorts, don't be talked out of them, but be aware of their limitations.

SHIRT

Two shirts are better than one. A T-shirt is light enough to avoid overheating while hiking on warm days. It can be exchanged for a warmer flannel, wool, or fleece shirt when camp is reached, or should the weather turn nasty. If it is really cool, both shirts can be worn. By having two shirts you can make the "layer system" work for you.

A heavier, warmer shirt should sport long sleeves and a collar. These features not only help with warmth, but also protect the arms and neck from sunburn and insects. Remember, skin burns easily at high altitudes. Should you go topless for a while, do it moderately. A sunburned back can be mighty painful when it's time to don packs again.

JACKET

Chances are, your jacket will be carried in your pack during the trek in. For this reason, you'll want one that's somewhat lightweight and not too bulky. Again, the material should breathe, and ideally lets moisture out but not in. Some fabrics, such as *Gore-Tex*, are especially designed to do just that.

You may decide on a fleece sweater or a sweatshirt instead of a jacket. That's fine. Probably the only disadvantage of sweaters is they are less water resistant than jackets. No matter which you choose, it can double nicely as a pillow for your bed; so keep it dry.

RAIN GEAR

The climate should dictate the type of rain gear to pack. If you expect heavy drenching rain, a full lightweight rain suit may be just the ticket. These outfits keep all outside moisture out, but also keep inside moisture from escaping. You wouldn't want to pursue strenuous tasks while wearing a full rain suit.

A more breathable and generally more practical alternative is the poncho. It permits air to flow in and out through side vents, and protects sufficiently from rain showers. Ponchos come in several styles and prices. Probably the ideal poncho is one designed especially for backpackers. It is long in the back so it can be draped over the pack as well as the packer.

I once commended Bradley how well he had fashioned a garbage bag into an economical poncho. He swiftly informed me, "It's not a [dang] garbage sack!" Ooh, I should be more careful with my compliments.

HAT

A hat is your shield from the sun and rain. A brimmed hat is effective for minimizing facial sunburn, especially the ears and nose. You may be exposed to long hours of intense sun rays, so wear your hat often, even when cloudy. Headgear should also be waterproof. Heads must be kept dry and warm to help avoid the possibility of hypothermia.

The head is the body's radiator, and your hat acts as its thermostat. Increase or decrease body heat using a hat. Keep it on during cooler moments, and take it off during hot sweaty hikes. If you are too hot with it off, soak the hat with cool water, and put it back on. Now your hat acts much like a swamp cooler or an old radiator bag used on the front of cars crossing a desert.

Before using a hat, try it on while wearing a backpack. Large brims in back may make annoying contact with the pack frame. If this is the case, you might as well find another suitable cap.

STOCKING CAP

If the weather sours, a stocking cap can be a real blessing. Worn beneath the hood of your poncho, it lends added warmth to sensitive ears. A more common use of a stocking hat is that of a night cap. Your entire body feels warmer inside your sleeping bag when your head and feet are kept warm. An exposed head can lose a lot of valuable body heat. Getting up in the morning is a little easier with the extra warmth a cap provides. Wear it during the cool morning hours until you are ready to face the day without it.

BANDANNA

We discussed some of the many uses of a bandanna in the chapter about equipment. A bandanna can also aid in keeping you warm. Wrapped loosely around your neck, it supplies additional insulation, much like a muffler.

CLOTHING ACCESSORIES

Try to stay dry! Wet clothing is uncomfortable and dangerous. Before each excursion, waterproof your pants, jacket, and hat with a water resistant spray. This won't replace the need for a poncho, but will help during a light rain shower, or when tromping through damp forests.

A small sewing kit may save the day. I once saw a fellow hiker (no, it wasn't Bradley) split the crotch in his only pair of trousers. This quickly became a breezy problem. A needle and thread was greatly appreciated. Monofilament fishing line can also be used, if you have a large needle along.

Last but not least on the clothing list is a pair of sunglasses. Some experts recommend two pair, in case one breaks. This is especially true when traveling in snow country, where bright reflections can cause temporary blindness. Even if you are not around snow fields, you still need sunglasses. Reduce eye strain by donning your shades whenever you are fishing, or are apt to be in direct sunlight for an extended period of time.

To summarize the subject of clothing, let's just mention a few general rules to follow. First, choose clothing that breathes. Perspiration can be as damaging as moisture from a rain storm, if not allowed to escape.

Use the layer system. Select several thin layers instead of a couple of thick ones. Then you can easily adapt to just about any climate, activity, or weather condition.

Make sure all clothes are in good repair. Since replacements are not available, you can ill afford faulty clothing. Double check all garments before your trip. Feel confident that each item will last the entire duration of your backpacking expedition.

7

Trail Techniques

Whoa, hold up a minute. Before starting the long trek into backpacker's paradise, let's make a few last minute adjustments. The making of a successful hike actually begins at the trailhead. What you do here may affect the outcome of the entire trip.

First, find a safe place to park your vehicles. Don't tear up the environment doing so. Use designated areas, so that from the beginning you are practicing low-impact camping. Most trailheads have a parking lot specifically for use by day hikers and backpackers. You may wish to park here, however, increasing outdoor crime has made it less attractive to do so. Consider parking next to a ranger station or in an actual campground space.

Campground fees are a cheap form of insurance. Your car is much less likely to be pillaged in a campground than at a trailhead parking lot.

Sad as it seems, thieves infest our National Parks and forests as well as our cities. They have discovered an easy mark in cars left unattended overnight at trailheads. It is discouraging to note this type of crime is rapidly increasing. Regardless of where you park, lock your car. Don't leave spare keys around your vehicle, and lock all valuables in the trunk, out of sight. Empty the glove box and leave it open, unless it activates a map light that drains the battery.

Beware of anyone loitering around the trailhead. One common ploy by thieves is to appear as another backpacker patiently waiting for someone. And he is! He's waiting for you. He'll watch you unpack, stash your valuables, and maybe even strike up a conversation with you, asking where you are going and for how long. Be ambiguous around suspicious characters and appear poor. If you really are poor, you're one step ahead of the crooks.

While still at the trailhead, several important tasks need attention. Now is the time to prepare your feet for the long hike ahead. Apply moleskin to areas susceptible to blisters. Pull socks up tight so there is no bunching inside your boots. Then make sure boots are snug and laces are tight.

If the weather is mild, you may wish to change into a T-shirt. You may be a little cool at first, but will quickly warm when hiking begins. It is better to be a little on the cool side than to wear a thicker shirt and sweat heavily.

Perspiration soaks clothes and causes rapid cooling during rest stops. Unless you are uncomfortably cold while hiking, save your heavier shirt until camp is reached. Then it will be a welcome change.

Limber up with a few light stretching exercises for your legs, back and shoulders. Even professional athletes stretch before each game, and they're in great shape. We would be wise to follow their example before slipping on our packs. Get ready for your big excursion; or should that be "big exertion?"

Members of your party may be arriving in different vehicles, and at slightly different times. Wait for everyone before starting to hike. Then you will know everyone at least got to the trailhead safely. Once everybody arrives, gather together and finalize the details of the trip. If you can predetermine who are the faster and slower hikers, divide into separate groups accordingly. Be sure each group has a map, and of course each person should have a compass. Specify when and where the groups plan to meet again. It is best to establish several checkpoints along your route. Good places to reunite are lakes, mountain passes, and especially any place where the trail forks. Meeting at the latter keeps each group from wondering if the other took the right path.

The trailhead is the place to once again check your equipment. See that nothing has fallen out of anyone's pack, and may be laying in the trunk of a car. Test all zippers, as well as cords that hold tents, sleeping bags, and pads to the pack frame. Cords and straps tend to loosen during a hike, so keep a close eye on them. It is very disheartening to reach camp and discover that somewhere along the trail lies a valuable piece of gear that fell from your pack. Help each other get packs on. Make sure packs fit comfortably before heading into the backcountry.

Many popular trails have registration forms at their heads. Take time to fill one out for your party. It may be helpful in locating you in case of an emergency. Registers also assist wildlife and forestry officials in measuring recreational use and environmental impact on a specific area. Supplying the data they need allows them to better serve us, the users, more effectively.

Now that we've covered the basic trailhead tasks, let's head on up the trail. It may seem that hiking consists of nothing more than walking. This might be true if you were raised in the mountains with a pack on your back, but for most of us it is an arduous feat. However, do not despair. Much of the fatigue and discomfort of backpacking can be minimized if a few simple tips are followed. Hiking can be pleasurable with the right mental attitude and the proper techniques.

A trekking pole is a solid investment in your safety and comfort. It is almost like having a third leg, allowing you to shift some of the burden from your legs to your arms. Walking sticks are most useful on steep grades and stream crossings. Whether wading a stream or balancing on a fallen log, a staff makes it easier and safer. It is surprising the additional balance a trekking pole offers. It may also come in handy for clearing brush or spider webs from your path, or fending off snakes.

Setting a comfortable pace is the single most important factor for an enjoyable hiking experience. Don't try to go faster than you feel good with. Over exertion is not only tiresome, but hazardous. Accidents happen more easily when you are fatigued, not to mention the risk of heart attack or heat exhaustion.

Chances are, members of your party will hike at different paces. Pair up with someone whose stride and physical abilities are similar to yours. Going too slow can be just as defeating as hiking too fast. Fast hikers should not be expected to slow down for those that lag behind, or perhaps wish to pause more to enjoy the scenery. Whether you are fast or slow, do not hike alone. You may need to alter your pace slightly to match another's if it means that otherwise someone hikes solo. This rule is easy to break during a long trek, so pay particular attention to it. It may save considerable grief.

Keep a comfortable distance between yourself and other hikers in your party. There is no need to be on someone's heels. A guy should have ample room to stop and look around, or tie a shoe without a fellow hiker bumping him. Besides, Bradley warns, "You wouldn't want a tree branch to slap ya in the face, would you?"

Long strides get you to your destination quicker than short ones. Take as long of a stride as feels natural, but don't force yourself to overstep. Put a little spring into your step, and you'll be moving along making good time.

There is a time and a place for short steps too. When conquering a steep hill, a series of small steps is easier than trying to gobble up ground with lengthy strides. Eventually the earth will level out; then resume your normal pace.

Another useful technique on uphill slopes is the "rest step." As each foot is placed forward, pause a second between when your forward foot is planted, and when you pull yourself up. This gives each leg a brief rest before any weight is put on it. Over the miles, these tiny rests add up to big energy savings, and help prevent muscle fatigue and leg cramps.

Rest stops are vital to a successful hike. How often you need to pause depends on your physical condition, the steepness of the slope, and the altitude. When you first start hiking you may feel like stopping after only a short distance. This is because your body is not warmed up yet. Don't stop now. Press on to obtain that all important "second wind."

When you decide to stop, make it count. The optimum length of time to rest is about five minutes. As you hike, your body builds up a waste called lactic acid. This waste makes you feel sluggish and weak. During a five minute break, thirty percent of lactic acid will be eliminated. Further resting will do little more to reduce it, and will probably make you more tired as muscles begin to stiffen.

Rest stops are a good time to check packs. Make sure nothing is falling out or coming loose. If a problem is discovered, take time to adjust it. Fix it better than it was before, otherwise it is likely to happen again, possibly without anyone noticing.

Backpackers often get into their packs during breaks. They may be after a quick energy snack, a canteen, a camera, a map, a cup, or a change of shirt or socks. Regardless of the reason, a good rule of thumb while on the trail is to only get one thing out at a time. Put it back before getting something else out. By doing this, you will be much less likely to overlook a valuable piece of gear once you strap on the pack and start hiking again. Oh, and don't forget to pick up any gear you may have been hand carrying.

If you have a fanny pack along, try wearing it with the pouch in front. This makes a handy place to store a camera, compass, map, sunglasses, water bottle, and snacks.

Don't wait for a rest stop to take a drink of water. As you hike, your body sweats away valuable minerals and fluids at the rate of one to two liters an hour. Frequent swigs from a canteen help maintain body fluid levels, preventing dehydration and fatigue. A cup every fifteen minutes would be about right. Carry at least enough water for half a day of hiking. If you wait until you are thirsty before drinking, you have waited too long.

Resist drinking from streams along the way. The water may appear crystal clear, but could contain giardia, which causes a serious illness often referred to as "backpacker's diarrhea", "beaver fever", or "Boy Scout trots." This parasitic bug is introduced into the water by waste from domestic livestock, beavers, dogs, or from dead animals. Unless you are positive what is between you and the water source, it is best left alone. Spring water is generally considered safe for drinking unless plants around it are dead or nonexistent. Other water should be boiled, then cooled before drinking.

Symptoms of dehydration include feeling irritable, confused, exhausted, nauseated, and of course thirsty. Dark yellow urine is an easily identifiable indicator. By losing 1.5 liters of water, your endurance may drop more than twenty percent. Lose three liters, and endurance levels are cut in half. Your body's ability to absorb oxygen also suffers when too much fluid is lost. So, to keep from feeling pooped-out, drink, and drink often.

To keep your energy up, munch on snacks as you go. Peanuts are excellent. They are loaded with quick releasing energy, and if salted, help replace lost body salts. Drink plenty of water with salty foods to curtail dehydration. Other good trail snacks include gorp, trail mix, raisins, and candies such as gum drops. Avoid messy chocolate goodies. However, you could get away with some of those candy coated chocolates that don't melt in your hand.

Maintain a comfortable body temperature throughout the hike. As mentioned in the clothing chapter, this is best accomplished using the layer system. By having an undershirt, T-shirt, long sleeve shirt, a jacket, and a hat, you can add or subtract articles as the weather dictates. Don't let clothing become saturated with sweat, or your body will cool too rapidly when you stop.

Alter your clothing often. When you first feel too cool or too sweaty is the time to make a change. Bradley reminded me, "You've covered this stuff about three times already." So I'll get off my soapbox and the subject of the layer system.

If overheating is a problem, cool down at lakes and streams along the way. Although streams may not be fit for drinking, there is nothing wrong with splashing your face, or soaking hot tired feet. Seasoned hikers find it refreshing to soak their bare feet awhile, and then slip on a clean pair of socks. This is a good idea at the midway point of a long trek.

Do your best to keep socks and boots dry. Soggy boots are weighty, not to mention cold and uncomfortable. Damp socks bunch up easily, which quickly leads to blisters. If a stream must be crossed, change into camp shoes without stockings on. Change back into boots after the danger of getting soaked is behind you. This *change over* is also effective when traveling through moist meadows or boggy areas.

Suppose you come to a river that is more than knee deep. If you have some extra rope, then you are prepared to cross. Locate a section of water that is straight, wide, and appears to be the shallowest. Next, try off a generous length of rope to a sturdy tree or large boulder that is just upstream from where you hope to cross. Now hold on tight to the other end of the rope, face upstream, and ease your way across the river. Keep the line taught as you go. *Do not tie the rope to yourself!* The current could hold you under if you are tethered to the rope and lose footing.

The question often arises (usually from novice hikers), "How close must I follow the trail?" The answer is simple. Stay on the trail as much as possible until your destination is reached. Although existing trails are not always the shortest distance between two points, it is the quickest and safest route. Even the smallest and most tempting shortcuts can be damaging to a hiker or the landscape. A good example is cross-cutting the trail between switchbacks on steep slope. You are much more likely to have a serious fall, and the new trail you start could lead to erosion of the hillside.

Another danger of leaving the trail is getting lost. Trails seldom twist and turn the way we anticipate. If you wander off the path with hopes of reuniting with it at a later point, chances are you won't find the trail where you expected it to be, if you find it at all.

Sometimes the trail may seem to disappear. This may happen at large meadows or rocky areas above timberline. Don't run off looking for the trail again. Instead look for trail markers. Tree blazes are common, and some areas now use small colored flags to prevent tree scars. Rock piles, called cairns, are used in places void of trees. When a ground trail is not visible, spot the next trail marker before pressing on.

Maybe the trail really does disappear, or you are exploring country with no established trails. In these cases you must rely heavily on a map and compass. Even when you have a good trail to follow, a map and compass help determine your current location, or verify you have not taken a wrong turn.

Hopefully you are using a detailed topographical map. With it and a compass, you can easily determine your approximate location using the following method. Use the compass to find which way is north. Then find the north end of the map (usually the top), and point it directly north. Now look around for two distant distinct landmarks that can be recognized on the map. With the map still pointing north, draw an imaginary line from each actual landmark through its spot on the map. Where the two lines intersect is your approximate location.

Three factors affect the accuracy of this method. The first is the detail and scale of the map. The more detailed, the better. Second is the degree of the angle between the two landmarks. Generally, the greater the angle, the more accurate your findings will be. Objects at 45-degree angles are ideal. The third factor is the distance of the landmarks from you. The further away, the more helpful. Good landmarks are mountain peaks, low spots in ridges, and small distant lakes.

Please keep the trailside clean! It should go without saying, don't litter. Nothing spoils the appearance of the wilderness quicker than scattered garbage. Even the smallest candy wrapper sticks out like a sore thumb. Most backpackers only carry food in burnable containers, so save the paper for campfire tinder. If trash cannot be burned, such as aluminum foil, pack it out. During the hike out, gather any litter left by other thoughtless hikers.

Human waste is another unsightly issue. When nature calls, get at least 200 feet from all trails and water sources. If you feel inclined to pee uphill, do so off to one side. Otherwise, gravity will force it right back, and you'll be standing in it. For pooping, it is advisable to dig a small "cat-hole" about six inches deep, and cover it when the paperwork is done. If only we could teach horses to do the same.

What are the guidelines when hiker meets horse on the trail? Sorry, the hiker must step aside. If the trail is crossing a slope, get off on the downside, allowing horse traffic to step on the more stable inside. Horses also feel less threatened when other animals (including people) are below them. Keep moving slowly, and talk. The horses will realize you're only human, and not some strange backwoods beast with a house on its back.

We have covered a lot of ground in this chapter. You may wish to review it just before your next outing. Tips and pointers given to aid you during the hiking in can be used during the trek out as well. One final rule when hiking out: wait for everyone to return to the trailhead. Don't drive away until you are sure every backpacker in your party is safely out of the woods.

8

A Backpacker's Camp

Aaaah, you've finally reached your destination, and now it's time to relax. Right? Not quite yet. First, camping accommodations must be arranged. There's no motel manager or maid service here, but the place makes up for it with exquisite atmosphere. The land is breathtaking and rugged. Some places are too rugged, or are less than ideal for a wilderness camp, so be selective when choosing a camp site. A lot of time and effort was expended getting here, now spend a little more locating the best spot to "hang your hat." If you are just stopping one night, you can afford to be less particular than if you're staying longer.

Allow plenty of time to choose and set up a suitable camp. Start your hike early enough that at least a couple hours of daylight remain once you arrive at your destination. If traveling in a large group, several small camps may be needed. Large camps are rarely available, and should be avoided to minimize impact on the environment.

The first decision to make is whether to make a new camp or to utilize an existing one. In high use areas, it is better to pick existing sites. Not only does less land scarring result, but there will be less work for you. Fire rings and cleared ground for tents already exist. All you need to do is move in.

Once a destination is reached, take off your pack. Then scout the area for the best campsite. If packs are left on, it is likely the first suitable camp encountered will be chosen, simply because you are tired. With burdens removed, searching for the best camp becomes an easy task. My destinations are often small lakes. I prefer to drop my pack near the lake, and walk around the perimeter, comparing all possible campsites as I go. Upon returning to my pack, I know where I want to pitch my tent. My pack and I walk directly to the right spot. You may prefer to check just one side of a lake, in which case you'll have the opportunity to compare sites a second time on the way back to your pack.

When choosing a campsite, give special consideration to a few desirable features. Level ground is necessary for a good camp. Pleasant sleeping calls for an even surface. Also, building a campfire on a slope is a poor idea. You wouldn't want gear rolling into the fire, or fire falling out of its designated area. Keep your camp on the level for safer, more comfortable camping.

Bradley's camping hint: "*?$?@* water runs downhill!" And he knows from experience. He once pitched his tent in a nice smooth site that just happened to be the lowest spot in camp. That night a storm rolled through, and Bradley soon had a waterbed. I can't tease him too much though, as I lost my rain fly once, and soon ended up with my own waterlogged bedding. Luckily this time Bradley had pitched his tent on high ground, and I slept in his tent. He snores.

Access to water is important when selecting your home away from home. A nearby spring is your best bet for liquid refreshment, but you could settle for a clean looking stream if you don't mind boiling your drinking water. It is surprising the amount of water one person uses. The closer the water supply, the less effort to fetch it. However, camp no closer than 200 feet to any water source, including lakes. This not only assures you won't inadvertently add pollution, but lessens the impact on the more fragile plant life growing nearby. This is just one of the rules of low-impact camping. The "200 foot" rule also applies to trails. Camp away from trails, and you'll be less noticeable to other hikers. You will also reap some rewards—more privacy and solitude. The mountain men of old practiced stealth for protection from others. We should do it today to limit intrusion.

If you are a non-fisherman, seek out fishless lakes to camp by. Odds are you won't have much company, and it's likely you won't see another soul. Peace and quiet can be found by anyone in quest of it.

Avoid damp or low areas. At night, these areas can be as much as fifteen degrees colder than ground slightly higher and dryer. The base of a steep mountain can be especially cold, as the night air rushes down the slopes. Depressed land in mountainous areas, called sinks, have long been known for their ability to produce record low temperatures. Camp a little ways up a hillside for warmer, more comfortable sleeping.

Camping among trees is the preference of most backpackers. Pines offer great protection from wind, sun and rain. You can often find a tent site with warm sun in the morning and shade in the hot afternoon. There are times however, when it may be beneficial to camp in the open. If mosquitoes are pesky, the wind brings welcome relief. Also, you may wish to have the warming sun on your camp all day. Autumn comes early to the high country, and with it, cooler temperatures.

Once a campsite is selected, section off four specific areas of use. These areas are: the kitchen, the sleeping quarters, the latrine, and the water supply. A latrine is optional and usually only recommended for large groups. Otherwise, campers can wander *way off* into the bush to do their duty.

The kitchen is the nucleus of the wilderness camp, and should be selected first. All other areas should then be chosen with safety, impact, and convenience in mind. In the kitchen, most activities center around the fireplace. Many times, fire rings already exist. If so, use them, although you may have to rearrange a few rocks to suit your needs. One of the best cooking fires is the keyhole, but you seldom inherit a fire ring set up this way. The keyhole is simply a round ring with an adjacent narrow slot, into which hot coals from the main fire can be shoved. Cook over the coals in the slot.

Set large logs and rocks around the fireplace for sitting. Small work counters can be fashioned out of flat rocks. Although low to the ground, they are handy during meal preparation. Do not build shelves or furniture using live trees. The pioneers may have done so, but those days have long passed. A comfortable and functional kitchen can be arranged while still keeping the low-impact spirit.

Protect food supplies from rummaging rodents. Hanging your cache from a shady tree is often sufficient. This practice becomes especially important in bear country. In this case, you may wish to suspend food high up a tree (about 10 feet), and a safe distance from camp. The food bag can be raised and lowered via a rope thrown over a secure branch. If bears are about, be sure all edibles are taken out of your packs, and certainly out of the tents. If a big bruin lumbers through camp, he is likely to leave packs and tents alone if no tempting scents are coming from them.

Bradley advises, "Also keep your hands washed of fish smell, or a bear might think you're lunch." I told him not to worry, at least until he actually catches a fish.

Another kitchen chore is dishwashing. Even this task should be done outside of camp when bears are around. One of the easiest methods to clean dishes is to fill the cook pot or pan with water and heat it. Add any plates, cups, and utensils. Let the dishes soak for a few minutes, then scrub with a plastic scouring pad. Dirty water and small (very small) food particles can be discarded behind a bush. Rinse with clean water. Let dishes air dry, or use a clean bandanna for a dish towel.

If fires are allowed, you'll probably want one in your kitchen. Even if cooking is done on a stove, a campfire provides warmth and a cheery atmosphere. Gathering and breaking firewood can be a huge job for one person, but if everybody pitches in for half an hour, enough wood can be stacked for a couple of days. Sticks of all sizes are needed, from cooking logs down to tinder. Since axes and hatchets are snubbed by sensible backpackers, look for dead dry wood that can be broken by hand or foot, or by throwing a large rock at the middle of a propped log. As you break wood, be mindful of flying pieces. You cannot afford an accident here.

Leave the green stuff alone. It's not much good for burning anyway. However, one of the best sources of tinder can often be found on the underside of large pine trees. Look for old snarls of dead twigs called "witches hair." It is especially useful after a rain storm. Much of the tinder on the ground may be soaked, but witch hair remains relatively dry. Boughs of dead (red) pine needles are another excellent fire starter.

One final note for the kitchen: Keep it clean! Don't become a slob in the great outdoors. Maintain a tidy camp by keeping gear and litter under control. A popular breakroom phrase sums it up pretty well. "Your mother doesn't work here, so clean up after yourself."

Sleeping quarters ought to be at least far enough from the kitchen to avoid hot sparks. These tiny "balls of fire" quickly burn holes in tents and sleeping bags. Even the most expensive bedding cannot repel a hot spark.

An unwise choice when selecting a tent site may have a long lasting impact on the environment. Don't pitch tents on any vegetation, grass included. Ironically, magazine advertisements by many tent manufacturers often depict people enjoying the wilderness with tents erected atop beautiful meadow grass. No wonder many campers get the wrong idea.

Find a site that is flat and dry. Nice places can be located beneath a canopy of medium size trees. Be cautious of the larger trees in the area. More than one backpacker has met his doom while resting under a tall tree in a lightning storm. Large rocks and tree roots are a nuisance, and should be shunned as a tent site if possible. Don't unseat large rocks, but feel free to clear any small stones and sticks from your sleeping area.

Camp away from dead trees that might fall during a wind, and rocky ledges that could choose to launch a boulder during the night. I, for one, would hate to see your sleep become permanent.

Drainage trenches should never be dug around tents. Trench scars last for years and are unnecessary. Choose a tent site that will not have water running through it during a heavy rain. One that slopes away from the tent would be ideal. Search under trees for sheltered, dry spots.

If you're an early riser, pitch your tent in a location where the morning sun can shine on it. By facing east, the warming rays make hopping out of the sack a little easier. Dawn is one of the prettiest times in the wilds, and is worth getting up for. Though, if you specifically want to *sleep in,* arrange bedding so that shady branches block the eastward facing.

Keep the area around your tent safe. Minimize the use of long cords. Those that are needed should be visible and not in high-traffic zones. Securing cords where they won't be tripped over may save someone a nasty fall, or save your tent from inadvertent collapse.

From your tent, the latrine should be situated so it can be found at night with the aid of a flashlight. This doesn't mean it has to be close, just accessible. Most latrines consist of nothing more than some designated bushes and a cat-hole. Cover each use with a small amount of dirt. The size of the hole depends on how many times you think it will be used. The number of people and the number of camping days are factors.

A small garden spade is practical for scooping out a new latrine. Leave it by the hole for shoveling dirt over waste. You may think it handy to always have toilet paper at your primitive commode. If so, a small empty coffee can laid on its side keeps paper dry.

The last major area of camp is the water supply. As stated earlier, it should be at least 200 feet away from the rest of your camp. If you are lucky enough to enjoy spring water, and it is coming out of a hillside, the following tip may prove to be a convenience. Slide a spare aluminum tent pole into the spring. Now you have constantly flowing, fresh tap water that can easily refill canteens. It beats dunking water containers in a shallow pool.

Boiling your water is one sure way to purify drinking water. Purification tablets may not kill all organisms unless directions are followed exactly. One in particular is giardia. This nasty parasite usually originates from animal waste, especially livestock and beavers. You really won't know if you ingest giardia until about a week later. Then you might get a severe flu-like disorder. It probably won't kill you, but you may wish that it would.

How about a shower? A plastic gallon milk jug weighs virtually nothing, and can be turned into a shower by punching several holes in the lid with a hot ice pick. Fill the jug, set it in the sunlight, and return later for a semi-luxurious warm shower.

Water for dishwashing and personal hygiene should be hauled away from the water source. Soaps are a terrible pollutant, and must not be introduced into wilderness waters. Food scraps also dirty the water, and are not to be washed into lakes and streams. Many foods are not as biodegradable as we might suppose. Everyone's help is needed to keep waterways clean.

Change into camp shoes. Heavy boots leave more of an impression than camp shoes, which are usually sandals or tennis shoes. A lot of wear-n-tear on a campsite can be saved just by wearing lighter footwear. Mother Nature thanks you, and your feet will too.

Low impact camping requires a constantly clean and organized camp. Garbage must be policed immediately, and not left to blow away. Clean all dirty dishes after each meal and return them to the pack. Keep gear and clothing neatly together, not strewn about camp or hanging from trees. There are benefits of a tidy camp. It will retain its sparkling wilderness appearance, and not that of an unkempt bachelor's apartment.

Everyone should share in the camp work. There are tents to pitch and firewood to gather. Routine chores like cooking, dishwashing, and water-fetching seem less ominous when each camper does his fair share. Don't take advantage of an individual who is willing to work. Jump in and help. You'll enjoy each other's company just as much working together as you will playing together. It's easy to spot the most ambitious person of the group. He is the one up first in the morning building a fire. Or maybe the poor guy just slept uncomfortably.

No doubt you'll be spending some time just sitting around camp. Large smooth rocks and logs work for stools, but what if you want a backrest? Just prop your pack against a tree or boulder, and sit back. The softness of this backrest depends on what is packed in the outermost compartments.

Since many seek the backcountry for its peace and quiet, maintain a quiet camp. This doesn't mean you need to whisper, but it is not the place for a loud party or excessive yelling. Low-impact camping consists of keeping noise pollution down, as you try to blend with the wilderness. It is surprising how far voices carry, especially across lakes, meadows, and canyons. If you have ever had noisy campers across the lake from you, then you know how it destroys any feeling of solitude. Practice a little stealth, and find your own piece of quiet.

Just as sure as you're reading this book, the time will come that most backpackers despise—the time to break camp. Whether you have been camping for several days or just overnight, care must be taken to restore the camp site to its natural state. Always leave a camp at least as good as you found it. If it was an existing site, odds are you'll be able to leave it in better condition than when you arrived.

The most important task of breaking camp is making sure the fire is out. Ashes must be cold to the touch, then could be lightly (very lightly) scattered about. If it can be avoided, do not cover the fire with dirt. Doing so only raises the level of the ring, possibly making it unusable by future groups.

Inspect the entire camp for litter. Even the tiniest scraps of paper should be packed out. Try to imagine what the backcountry would look like if every visitor left just one candy wrapper that was never picked up. It wouldn't take too many years for the scenery to diminish.

Looking for a worthwhile project? Arrange with the proper authorities to clean an area. Gather all trash left by others, put it in garbage bags, and cache it where it can be later removed by a ranger. What a great way to beautify the environment without having to pack out someone else's mess.

Gather absolutely all your gear. Care needs to be taken when repacking your pack. It was probably stuffed when you arrived, and now you need to make it all fit again. The only thing missing will be the food eaten during your stay. All the guidelines for packing in apply when preparing to "bug out" or move on to another camp. You'll be tempted to haphazardly stuff your gear into your pack and head down the trail. But do yourself a favor. Organize and balance the pack for comfortable hiking, and double check that all tents, sleeping bags, pads, and fishing poles are secured.

Restore the land to the condition you found it. If you cleared the ground of twigs and pine needles, scatter some over the bare soil. Reseat any large rocks you unearthed during your stay. If you built a new camp site, make particular efforts to restore the area to its natural setting. You may even go so far as to erase footprints by brushing the dirt with a bough of pine needles.

Camp restoration is an extremely important aspect of low-impact camping. If everyone does his or her part, we can keep our pristine wilderness for generations to come. The land is not ours to abuse, it is ours to preserve. We need to assure our children inherit the same outdoor opportunities we enjoy.

9

High Country Fishen'

You may have just asked the question, "What does fishing have to do with backpacking?" If you did, you can probably save yourself some time and skip this chapter entirely. For some, fishing is not even a consideration when backpacking, but for others it is the primary reason they come to the high country. If you are one of these happy addicts, or if you just want to catch a few trout for the pan, then read on. Fishing the backcountry is probably much different than what you're used to, so you're going to want a few pointers. Entire books are available on high country trout fishing, but here we'll just summarize some good sound basics.

Understanding how high country trout live, and what they eat can mean the difference between getting skunked and catching your limit several times over. One such instance comes to mind. We had just hiked twelve miles into Farmer's Lake located in Utah's High Uinta mountains. A Boy Scout troop was just preparing to hike out. We asked, "How's the fishen?" Their reply was, "Lousy! We only caught two between all of us, using worms and salmon eggs." Well that deflated my hopes, but I was about to learn a valuable lesson. Give the fish what they are used to eating—bugs, small bugs. The very next morning all four members of our party caught and released over fifty brook trout each. Any tiny fly coaxed an orange-bellied brookie from its hideout. Sometimes the pattern doesn't matter, but size almost always does.

Size 16 and smaller. Got it? Let me repeat. Size 16 and smaller. I've lost track of how many fellow fishermen I have told this to, but somehow they forget the advice once they reach the tackle shop. Psychologically, I think people talk themselves out of purchasing small flies. Maybe it's because they don't believe they are getting much for their money. Perhaps they don't think a trout will attack something so tiny, and if it did, how could the small hook hold a decent fish? Believe me, these itty-bitty balls of feather and fur are just the ticket for high country trout, big or small.

Why do the fish prefer such a small tidbit? Answer: because that is what they are used to eating. Most mountain trout never see a worm, nor do they ever see the likes of grasshoppers, beetles, or large terrestrials. Midges comprise from 60 to 90 percent of an alpine trout's diet. That's a fact that cannot be ignored if you expect to consistently catch trout in lakes above 10,000 feet.

Now, how do you fish such a small offering? If you are an accomplished fly-fisherman, you already know the answers. But if you're not, such is my case, then let me suggest the bubble and fly method. This technique is more widely used than traditional fly fishing due to its simplicity. If you can spin cast, you can catch fish using a bubble and fly. To rig your line, start with a one-inch clear plastic bubble about two-thirds full of water. Thread the bubble onto your line, and attach a snap swivel to the end of the line. Next, measure off about three to four feet of four-pound test leader. Attach one end to the swivel, and the other to a fly. Now you're all set. Simply cast out, then reel in slowly; maybe even slower. In calm water, you should notice a slight wake coming from the bubble as it slides through the water—in choppy water, no wake at all. The fly will naturally ride a couple of inches below the surface, which is right where you want it. This "feeding zone" is where cruising trout find most of their meals. They prefer bugs under the surface because less energy is spent inhaling an insect than plucking it off the top.

Some fishermen avoid the bubble and fly method because they believe the splash of the bubble scares the fish. This may be true if you cast directly on top of risers, but try casting beyond trout holding areas, then dragging your fly over waiting fish. I have seen the initial splash of the bubble actually act as an attractor. Fish often mistake the splash as that of another feeding fish, and move in quickly to get their share of grub.

There are several advantages of the bubble and fly technique over conventional fly fishing. (1) There is no troublesome back-cast. This becomes important on many alpine lakes surrounded by "fly eating" conifers. (2) Casting distance can be double that of fly fishing. This is a critical factor on shallow lakes, or when trying to reach a feeding zone from a side angle. I have seen casting distance make the difference between catching many fish or none at all. (3) It is easy to switch to using spinners. With minor changes in tackle, you can quickly be fishing deep holes with your favorite lure.

Spinners are not to be forgotten either. Although flies are the main course, high country trout will often chase a well-presented piece of hardware. There are very few minnows in high lakes, but fish will smack a lure if they're in the mood for a fight, especially the real lunkers. If flies aren't producing, switch to lures, and fish them deep. Best sizes are 0 thru 2. If you are planning on releasing the fish, change your lure's hooks to either single or barbless. Barbed treble hooks are murder on released trout. Bend barbs down with needle-nose pliers to make hook removal quicker and less damaging. Also, play the fish quickly so that it has enough energy to swim away on its own. Avoid touching released fish, but if you have to, wet your hands to prevent the removal of the protective mucous (slime).

Have you ever found yourself wanting a lure, and you don't have any around? Well, here's a *cheap trick* to remember for such an occasion. Just mold some tin foil around a plain hook, so that it shimmers and wiggles when it's drug through the water. This may also prove to be a note-worthy survival technique.

Streams are the best place for devout spin fishermen. High country brooks can be loaded with pan-sized trout that find a spinner irresistible. Meandering meadow streams are ideal for locating eager fish as they hide in the shadows of undercut banks, waiting for their next meal to float by. Approach mountain streams cautiously, light-footed, and with a low profile. Let these wary trout see or hear you, and you might as well forget it.

Beaver dams along streams are an excellent bet for finding schools of fish. Then again, depending on the age of the dam, you may find nothing. The newer the dam, the better the fishing is likely to be. Older dams tend to become silt laden, and lose their food producing capabilities. Trout soon move out of these sterile areas. But if there's lots of food around, so will there be fish. Treat beaver dams as miniature lakes. It may be wise to switch back to using a fly on these slow stretches of water. This is where a real fly fisherman will have the advantage, as a bubble does tend to spook wary beaver dam trout. Because these trout see more natural predators such as beaver and otter, they tend to be much more alert than fish in larger reservoirs or fast moving streams. One quiet technique for fishing small ponds is to cast to the opposite shore, then gently drag the bubble and fly into the water, thus eliminating any noisy splash.

It is important to approach even large lakes carefully. When coming upon a new body of water, move slowly and quietly towards the shore. High country trout are often in shallow water near the water's edge. If they spot you, they may be gone for quite a spell. I have caught large cutthroats just three feet from shore by just dunking my fly in the water in front of a cruising fish. These instances also taught me the importance of wearing neutral-colored clothing. Had I been wearing bright clothes, I seriously doubt my luck would have been as good. Fish distinguish colors very well, as proven by their occasional finicky disposition when only the right fly pattern will do.

When trying out a new lake, always work the shallows first for cruising trout. Good areas to start with are inlets, outlets, and the shoreline casting into the wind. All three are great collectors of bugs (fish know this too). Check out the insects on the water. Then see what you have in your fly box that most closely resembles them. "Matching the hatch" is the quickest way to determine what the fish may be feasting on that day. If there is no apparent hatch, begin your search for fish with an attractor pattern. A Renegade or something with a subdued orange or olive green body often gets their attention.

If it's spawning season, try a salmon-egg fly near inlets or shallow gravel beds. This is an excellent opportunity to pick up some of the lake's older residents, as they lose their wary nature. Like most wildlife, they are most vulnerable when their reproductive organs are most active. Do yourself a favor. If you do catch a nice spawning trout, release it. The rewards will be reaped for years to come. An exception to this might be if you are catching stunted fish, as is common with brook trout.

Stunted trout are easily recognized by their proportionally large heads contrasted by a skinny body. Brook trout are such prolific reproducers, they often over-populate. If you find such a place, enjoy the lightning fast fishing, then have yourself an old fashioned fish fry. It will improve the health of the remaining stock if some of the competition is harvested.

Most often it will not be spawning season however. So as mentioned, begin working the shallow sections of the lakes. If these areas prove unproductive, move to deeper water. Look for areas where the lake bed drops off sharply into a deep pool. Cast along the drop-off line. Fish like the safety of the deeper water, but will venture away long enough to grab a quick-and-easy meal. Large submerged rocks and trees are great fish holding areas that should be given special consideration. Places where food and safety are handy are prime real estate for trout.

When to fish is just as important in the high country as it is on the lowlands. Early morning, just as the sun warms the shallows, is the best time for fast fishing. A close second is the late evening about a half hour before sunset. Too many anglers make the mistake of hiking into an area during the productive morning hours, fishing during midday, then hiking out in the late afternoon. Then they wonder why the trout weren't biting. Admittedly, time of day does not matter on some alpine lakes. They are good all day long. But most lakes will have their feeding times, most likely in the early AM or late PM. Concentrate your serious fishing around these times, especially for the big ones.

Weather is often a factor, but not in the way you might expect. Bad weather often brings good fishing. If the winds are blowing or rain is falling, don't head for shelter, start casting. Wind and rain force more bugs in the water, and the fish may respond with feeding frenzies. Large trout are susceptible during bad weather as they attempt to consume large amounts of insects while expending little energy.

Another advantage of nasty weather is that the water's surface is distorted, and so is the appearance of your fly. Selective trout cannot tell an artificial from a real insect in rough water, and will smack a fly that wouldn't pass inspection under calm conditions. I recall one particular instance at Fire Lake when the water was literally boiling with trout feeding on a flying ant hatch. My imitations drew barely more than a casual glance until a breeze rippled the surface. Then I could catch three or four hungry cutthroats before the water stilled again. All I could do was patiently wait for the next gust of wind.

Before and after storm fronts are exceptional fishing periods. Fish sense a change in barometric pressure, which rings their dinner bell. As storms come and go, winds blow insects out of the air and into the water. The abundance of food, coupled with instincts that tell fish it may be a while before another good meal, set trout on an active search for food. In this mood, they seldom slow down long enough to inspect a fly before engulfing it. Action may be fast and furious just before the brunt of a squall hits. If not equipped with good rain gear, you may be wise to wait out the storm, or at least its initial blast.

How do you find a good fishing hole? The best advice I can give is to camp in an area surrounded by several lakes. If one doesn't pay off, hike over to the next lake. The majority of high country lakes are small in size and generally located within walking distance of others.

Prospecting for "hot" lakes is a very enjoyable aspect of high country fishing. You'll feel a great deal of personal satisfaction when you discover a lake that yields a battling cutthroat on nearly every cast. Or maybe your search will end at a remote glacier-fed lake harboring a few old monarchs that have never seen an artificial lure, until they attack yours.

Check out places other fishermen would probably bypass. Small streams or ponds connected to lakes often hold a surprise or two. Inaccessible or *hard to find* lakes receive far less angling pressure than those along the trail, and their treasures are usually worth the extra effort. It's amazing how the fishing improves once you get off the beaten path. Remember to approach remote waters cautiously. These shy trout are not accustomed to visitors.

Do your homework. Much searching can be done long before your trip. Study maps, and locate a likely group of lakes not in a high use area. Topographical maps are available at the nearest Geological Survey office. Booklets or pamphlets detailing lake characteristics and stocking plans may be obtained from local Fish and Game departments. Most major mountain systems have books written about hiking their trails.

Some are specifically written with the backpacking fisherman in mind. Gather all the material you can before deciding when and where to base your fishing adventure.

"Word of mouth" is a valuable resource. Talk it up with friends, fellow workers, and even casual acquaintances such as the barber. Someone has likely heard the bragging of a successful fisherman who was more than willing to share his tale. But be careful of liars. More than one angler has been known to stretch the truth.

Speaking of stretching the truth, some professional guides do just that. If you're not familiar with an area, you may be wise to seek the expertise of a guide. A good guide can save you valuable time in exchange for some valuable money. However, check out a guide's reputation before placing your money and trip in his hands. Any guide worth his salt should be able to provide you with a list of references of satisfied customers. Call them. See if the experience they had is the kind you're looking for. Most guides are good guides, but as in any profession there are a few bad apples spoiling the general image.

Well I've said about enough on high country trout fishing, except that I haven't found anything that compares with it. The action is frequently fast, and the scenery is always magnificent. It gets in your blood, and you'll want to go back for more and more, year after year. Just one last friendly reminder, *size 16 or smaller.*

10

Have a Safe Trip

"**An ounce of prevention** is worth a pound of cure."
I don't know who originally coined this popular phrase,
but he/she would have made a darn good backpacker. A
single statement couldn't have more truth than this one
as it applies to backpacking. If it isn't a hiker's slogan, it
ought to be, and perhaps *"safety first"* should be our
motto.

We've already hashed over the idea that we need to
avoid any activity or equipment that may lead to an
accident in the backcountry. Being many foot miles away
from medical attention can turn a simple accident or
illness into a life threatening situation. All safety
precautions must be strictly adhered to.

Choose your backpacking buddies as carefully as you do your gear. Anyone who is careless or likes to take unnecessary risks, probably won't make a good hiking partner. Even if this person only hurts himself, it would ruin your trip if you have to care for him, or go for help.

I mentioned at the beginning of this book that Bradley was a rebellious and rough guy, but did I mention that he's reckless? No, because he isn't, and I'm grateful for that. Over the many years we've backpacked together, I have never witnessed Bradley being careless, unless you count bonfires. Nor has he had any accidents. In fact he can tease me about an accident I once had while rock hopping across a boulder field. I tumbled and slid over some huge rocks, and miraculously only managed some nasty scrapes and torn clothes. My fishing pole didn't fare as well, as it disappeared down between the boulders. To this day I hate boulder fields, and will plan my routes meticulously to avoid them. And Bradley knows it.

There are many fine books written about first aid, but this isn't one of them. In the interests of brevity and keeping with our slogan, this chapter will only deal with "an ounce of prevention." It is important to know what the potential dangers of the backcountry are, how to recognize them, and how to elude them. First aid training is recommended, but even more important is learning how to prevent trouble.

Hazards abound in the wilderness. Like a deadly enemy, they may sneak up on you slowly, or strike with sudden brutal force. Most people perceive backcountry trouble to be of the "sudden" variety, such as lightning.

However most trouble comes about slowly, with unpreparedness, fatigue, ignorance, and carelessness being contributing factors.

Hypothermia is the number one killer of campers. Not bears, not lightning, not snakes—hypothermia! The lowering of the body's core temperature is extremely lethal, and can happen without hardly noticing the initial signs. Shivering and clouded thinking mean it is time to take action before it's too late. If you expect hypothermia is upon you, start warming up immediately. A warm fire helps, as will hot liquid drink. Bundling up in blankets will not reverse hypothermia because your body cannot reheat itself. Heat must come from an external source. In extreme cases it may be necessary for another person to strip down and get into a sleeping bag with the victim. Using another's body heat is an excellent way to gradually and safely warm a hypothermia candidate.

Any combination of two out of three factors can lead to hypothermia. Water, wind, and cold are the three deadly ingredients. Put any two of them together, and you're asking for trouble—slow trouble. Warm dry clothing is the key to preventing hypothermia from sneaking up on you. Take all necessary precautions to remain dry. Rain gear is a must, and be especially protective of your head. A cold wet head loses heat faster than any other body part.

Another slow killer is heat stroke. Hyperthermia is the opposite of hypothermia. The body can overheat as the result of dehydration, exertion, and hot temperatures. The best ways to dodge hyperthermia is to drink plenty of fluids and limit strenuous activities when temperatures are soaring. Muscle cramps are a sign of dehydration and warrant immediate attention. Lots of water with an occasional salt tablet should remedy the situation.

Dehydration is a common occurrence among backpackers, even when the weather is mild. We tend to forget to drink the extra water our bodies need to replace fluids lost by sweat. Some of the less critical but uncomfortable symptoms of dehydration are constipation and chapped lips. It really pays to keep lots of water aboard.

Pushing yourself to the point of fatigue is dangerous. Fatigue itself presents no physical hazard, but the accompanying tired muscles and slow thought processes make accidents more probable. As legs turn to rubber, they no longer lift as high as they should. Before long you might be "shuffling" along, ready to trip and fall over an unexpected tree root that has chosen to parallel the surface. A fatigued mind is a slow reacting mind. It may not respond quickly enough to escape an accident. Many accidents wouldn't even happen if the victim had responded a half a second sooner. Keep yourself perky by replenishing your energy with plenty of snacks, water, and rest stops.

Shortcuts can be perilous. Trails were made for a reason. Getting off the trail, even to just cut across a switchback, can lead to a catastrophe. Maybe you'll tumble down a mountainside, or get into treacherous terrain that forces you to back track. Perhaps you'll get lost. Inexperienced hikers die every year because they got lost, panicked, and were overcome by the unforgiving elements of nature. Stay with the trail for a safer, easier journey.

"Getting in a hurry" is probably the chief cause of accidents in the backcountry. It is a common mistake to plan on covering more miles than you can manage. Map miles are measured "as the crow flies." I have never seen a mountain trail yet that went straight from point A to point B. They always twist and turn, go uphill and down, until you usually have hiked almost double the map distance. Plan on hiking about one and a half miles per hour. This is a quick, but comfortable pace for mountainous terrain.

Allow yourself ample time to reach your destination, otherwise you may find yourself getting in a hurry. And that's where the danger lies. The harder you push on, the sooner fatigue will overcome, and the more apt you are to stumble and fall, take a wrong turn, or lower your body's resistance to the elements.

Have you ever heard of altitude sickness? Did you think it was a myth? Well, it's not. It is very real, and about 100 people die from it each year. Altitude sickness affects only a slight percentage of people, but is a major discomfort and danger for them. Unfortunately the only treatment for it is to go back down. If altitude sickness is a potential problem, then limiting your ascent to 1,000 feet per day will usually allow you to escape illness.

Let's talk about one more form of slow trouble, then we'll discuss some of the gory, quick-killing hazards you've been waiting for. Sunburn, ah yes, the dreaded sunburn is a discomfort many endure. But it doesn't have to be that way. Sunburn is the easiest of all natural hazards to prevent. Simply keep susceptible areas such as your neck, ears, nose, back, and legs covered with clothing or sunblock. Collared shirts and wide brimmed hats are invaluable to a backpacker exposed to countless hours in the great outdoors. Wear your hat even when it's cloudy. You are probably well aware that the sun's rays that cause burning go right through thin clouds.

Sunburned eyes, referred to as snow-blindness in extreme cases, is preventable. Sunglasses are indispensable in the high country. Wear them whenever the sun is bright, or when you are facing snow or water glare. Again, a good hat will aid eye protection. I mentioned earlier that your feet are the most important part of your body to take care of, because they take you everywhere you need to go. Let me retract that statement. Your eyes are most important. You obviously aren't walking anywhere if you suddenly can't see where you're going.

What's the *numero uno* danger shelled out by the weather in our world today? Let me give you a hint. Just before it hits, the hair on the back of your neck rises. If you feel such a sensation while hiking, drop to the ground immediately and place your head lower than your hip. You might be struck by lightning! By lowering your head and torso you may direct the brunt of the shock away from your head and vital organs, hoping it hits you in the butt, then goes through your legs to reach the ground.

Lightning strikes about one thousand people in the United States each year. Three hundred of those die. Many others are severely burned or otherwise injured. To dodge becoming one of these statistics, obey the following rules: During lightning storms stay off peaks and ridges, avoid the tallest trees, don't let yourself become the highest point around, stay out of water, shun damp caves, and get away from the metal tubing of backpacks and tents. The best advice is to shed your backpack and wait out the electrical storm beneath a group of small trees.

Injuries inflicted by wildlife are probably the most publicized of wilderness mishaps. We've all heard horror stories about wolves, bears and snakes, but animal incidents constitute a small percentage of outdoor deaths. Thanks to media hype, we perceive wild animals to be a more prevalent danger than they really are. Not that some critters aren't dangerous (they are), but we may be misled to believe that animal incidents are common place, which they are not.

However, precautions should be taken to avoid contact with the real beasts of the wilderness. Hiking is not the time to practice your stealth. Make noise freely and often. Wild animals don't want a human encounter, and will flee the area long before your arrival, if they know you are coming.

Bears are known trouble makers, but be aware of less threatening looking animals as well. The moose is a classic example. Most often a moose appears docile and unconcerned with passing humans. But if for any reason a moose feels threatened, it can be every bit as dangerous as a grizzly bear. In fact, a mature bull moose will usually win a scuffle with a bear.

Store food away from tents. If bears are a potential hazard, then suspending food in a bag well up a tree may prevent an unfortunate incident. And by all means don't make yourself appear as a tasty morsel by storing food in your pockets. A bear's keen sense of smell goes right through snack wrappers.

Now let's talk about some less dangerous but bothersome creatures of the animal kingdom, those pesky bugs. Remember the mosquito repellent! It may not affect your safety, but most certainly will be a comfort factor, unless of course you are blessed enough to go backpacking during a season when the "skeeters" are inactive. In case you are unaware, mosquitoes in the backcountry are often horrendous. They swarm about in clouds, attracted to any animal that promises blood. In extreme cases, mosquito netting for your face is needed, but not often.

Let me divulge Bradley's secret weapon for warding off mosquitoes—a cigar. This was discovered by accident during our wild teen years. We had hiked into a fairly wet area that harbored the most ferocious mosquitoes I have ever come across. Even with two brands of repellents applied liberally to our skin and clothing, they practically smothered us as they swarmed in our faces, flew in our mouths, and buzzed in our ears with their irritating high pitched whine. Being "smart" as teenagers are, we had brought along cigars to show how cool and independent we were. We felt amazed and relieved to discover the effect cigar smoke had on the seemingly endless supply of mosquitoes. Poof! One puff and they were gone. I mean they weren't even in sight. Guess it made them sick too. I've since given up cigars, as I've learned to dodge the large hordes of mosquitoes located in wet areas.

What you eat can affect your popularity among mosquitoes. Bananas, even eaten a couple days earlier, cause your body to emit an odor very favorable to biting bugs. According to a good friend of mine, garlic has an opposite effect. "Munch a clove of garlic and mosquitoes are history," he says. I haven't personally tested this theory, but I believe it could work. Mosquitoes won't be the only creatures getting out of your way.

Another fearsome insect is the tick. What I can't figure out is how some rock hard bug can burrow into my skin without me feeling a thing. But they can. Ticks can carry severe illnesses such as Lyme's disease or Rocky Mountain Spotted Fever. These disorders won't be noticed on your hike, unless it's a long one, but could adversely affect your health for months, even years, to come.

Examine your body regularly for invading ticks. Look especially close at warm unexposed areas such as under arms, between legs, the neck, and around your waist where a belt is worn. Should an embedded tick be found, coax him to relax his grip by applying stove gas, mosquito dope, or sun tan lotion. Then extract the pest with tweezers, grasping the head if possible. Do not squeeze the tick's body, which might force its infectious stomach contents into your bloodstream. You really need to get the little sucker to back out before applying pressure.

When poisonous plants are mentioned, what comes to mind? Is it those three leaf shrubs that irritate the skin, or is it wild plants that can make you sick upon ingestion? Either type is a definite hazard to steer clear of, but the latter can give you the most grief, and possibly kill you. A lengthy discussion about edible vegetation is not necessary or appropriate for this publication, so let's just make a rule about which wild plants we can eat— none. Leave them all alone! Unless you are a so called "expert" on edible plants, it is best to refrain from eating any plant life found in the backcountry. Although wild raspberries are hard to pass up, so I eat them.

Think about the more common ailments of backpackers. The most common one I can think of are blisters. These water-filled skin bubbles cause more pain more often than any other single type of injury or illness. As prevalent as they are, blisters are still easily preventable. Thick tight socks are highly recommended for good foot health. Thickness reduces friction on the foot, while tightness prevents bunching up. Wherever a sock can wad up is a potential spot for a nasty blister. Keeping socks dry and changing them often adds longevity to elasticity, keeping them tight.

Probably the most common cause of blisters isn't sloppy fitting footwear, but boots that are too tight. Boots should allow your feet to slide around a bit. It's not the sliding that creates blisters, but the constant sudden stopping and cramming at the end of the slide. By loosening boots a little, your feet can move without heel and toe jamming. Be sure you know how to adjust the fit of your boots "just right." I think my favorite footwear statement warrants mentioning again. Your feet are the only means of transportation you have. Care for them accordingly.

Okay, let's assume you've followed all of the above rules, and taken the necessary precautions, but the odds have caught up with you, and now you have a serious injury. What do you do? I hope you can readily see the risks of solo hiking. Break your leg while hiking alone, and you may soon be pushing up daisies. But for our case, let's assume we were wise enough to have a couple of sensible hiking companions.

It's easy to reason that an injured or ill person must get out of the backcountry as soon as possible, and seek real medical attention. What is the quickest, most feasible way out? In most cases the sufferer can be assisted out by his buddies. Slings, splints, crutches, a travois, or even a litter can be constructed from raw materials at hand. If the victim can be moved, and the terrain is passable, then I would attempt to help the unfortunate hiker "out of the woods."

Extreme cases warrant rescue. If professional aid or gear is needed, send someone for help. Send two if you can, but do not leave the victim alone. Somebody must attend the victim to keep him comfortable, or in case conditions worsen and further aid is needed.

It is apparent the wilderness is a dangerous place if a person is unaware of how to avoid various hazards. And perhaps we need more than an ounce of prevention. A pound is more like it. We need to become more cautious once we step into the backcountry, and begin playing a new game of life. The rules are set by nature. They are never the same, nor fair, and they respect no one. Have a safe trip!

11

Not Bankruptcy

Pun intended. Just as Chapter Eleven doesn't have to mean bankruptcy, backpacking doesn't need to be expensive. On the contrary. A backpacking trip can be the least expensive type of vacation to plan. It might even be cheaper than staying home. Get in touch with nature, without losing touch with your money.

Even if you're not an avid camper, you'll likely have many backpacking provisions around the house. A look through your garage, kitchen, bedroom, and storage areas should turn up a large percentage of the equipment, food, and clothing needed for a few carefree days on the trail.

Remember, some gear can be used for multiple purposes. Also, most necessities can be suitably replaced by things you already have at home, or by equipment that is less expensive than what is so often suggested. Below is a quick and dirty summary of alternative gear. For additional substitutions, or if you would like further explanation of the ones listed, refer back to chapter three. I am not saying these alternatives are better, just alternatives, and often less costly.

Please go to the next page to see the list.

Need	Substitute
Waterproof matches	wax dipped matches
Waterproof match container	empty aspirin bottle
Trail mix	bulk ingredients, mixed
Sleeping bag liner	old bed sheet
Backpacking sleeping bag	regular sleeping bag
Backpacking pad	½ - 1" foam pad
Duffle bag	garbage bag
Canteen	sturdy water bottle
Flashlight	disposable flashlight
Toothbrush	make one from a willow
Extra shoes	tennis shoes
Poncho	cut-out garbage bag
Plate	paper plates
Spoon, fork	from the kitchen
Cup	measuring cup
Tent	thick drop cloth
Map	photocopy of original
Pot	metal can with a wire
Scour pad	soft pinecone
Stove	firewood at camp
Tackle box	sealable plastic bag
Fish creel	plastic bag with a twist tie
Multiple tool	small needle-nose pliers
Clothing repair kit	safety pin
Soap	liquid dish soap
Hot-pad, towel, bandage	bandanna
Day pack	clothing with large pockets
Stretch bandage	athletic sock without foot
Moleskin	duct tape
Camp shower	plastic milk jug
Fire starter	1-inch sq. of inner tube

As you can see, many of the substitutions can be found around the house, or can be bought at the supermarket or hardware store at a fraction of the cost of the "real thing." Many alternatives have disadvantages or trade-offs. You'll need to measure these, and decide for yourself what you are willing to live with while backpacking. If equipment cost is a major issue for you, then several minor inconveniences can to be tolerated.

Army/Navy Surplus outlets or thrift stores are dandy places to pick up new or used supplies. Used gear may be uglier than new gear, but it's a lot cheaper. Anyway, after one backpacking excursion it's tough to tell if an item was new or used before you started. Beware of some of the bulky army gear. It was never designed with weight in mind, and may be heavier than you want to carry. Military equipment was meant to be durable, and should last many moons. Army/Navy outlets often stock tents, sleeping bags, foam pads, cooking kits, external packs, day packs, canteens, stoves, pocket knives, hats, shirts, jackets, gloves, trousers, underwear, and socks. They even have boots, but these are not too good for backpacking. I would buy my boots elsewhere.

Keep backpacking in the back of your mind throughout the year. Be on constant lookout for samples and trial-size products that might be ideal for packing. Samples are often free, trial sizes are cheap, and both are lightweight. The mail, restaurants, and hotels are prime locations for finding mini backpacking supplies.

Once all of your equipment is acquired, backpacking becomes much less expensive on subsequent trips. It's possible that the only cost required is for food and gas. I have taken a four day excursion for a mere twenty dollars. By sharing meals and transportation, the cost per hiker becomes minimal. If only I could live four days at home and thoroughly enjoy myself for twenty bucks.

Don't convince yourself that your gear will last forever. The rough wilderness takes its toll. Double check your stuff before each trek, and replace any questionable items. I usually pick up gear throughout the year when I spot it on sale. Then I don't have any prohibitive expenses when it comes time to backpack. This may seem like I'm hiding some costs. Well, I guess I am.

Remember the chapter about what not to take? "Don't take" also means "don't buy." Forget about the more expensive and heavier equipment that wise backpackers don't even include in their inventory.

Beginners to the sport of backpacking should take a serious look at renting some of their equipment. Rent gear similar to what you might later buy, and see if it's what you really want. Often times, first impressions are not correct, and having the opportunity to field test equipment can save you from making a costly mistake. Commonly rented gear includes tents, sleeping bags, packs, and stoves.

Fishing tackle can be a formidable expense if you let it. I used to take along a large assortment of flies and lures, thinking I would surely have something the trout would inhale regardless of their mood. After a few trips, I realized that I was almost always using a few select flies and spinners that had become my personal favorites. Find out what works! Carry a generous supply of the "hot" lures, and don't waste money or pack space on the many odd balls.

Budget tip: Have fresh fishing line wound onto your reel at a sporting goods store. They often feature this service. The cost is usually half that of buying comparable line and winding it yourself. Fresh, stretchable line is vital for maximizing casting distance, and once a nice fish is hooked, pliable line is much less likely to break.

Now let's assume you actually manage to catch a fine mess of fish. Is it a free lunch? Yes and no. You already spent hard earned cash for fishing tackle and a license, but that expense was hopefully budgeted under the category of "recreation." Look at fresh trout as a bonus or side benefit, since you had to shell out the money whether you caught anything or not. Although you'll probably never eat enough fish to pay for your fishing related costs, a meal of *free* fried fish soothes and satisfies any budget-minded gourmet.

Please keep only enough fish for your next meal. They won't stay fresh in the backcountry any longer than that. Releasing most trout ensures a good fishery for years to come, while wasteful anglers can decimate a wilderness lake in a single season. Need some proof for bragging rights? Take photos instead of fish. Pictures last much longer than fish. Release your shutter, then the fish, but go ahead and save a couple for dinner.

What about the rest of the meal? How can we keep expenses down while specializing in lightweight, dried foods? Easy! Remember the supermarket tactics discussed in an earlier chapter. There is no need to venture any further than the local market to obtain the nutritional necessities of a backpacking excursion. Costly freeze-dried packet meals may be practical for a full-fledged expedition, but for 95% of us backpackers they are too expensive when compared with the many entrees, side dishes, and snacks offered in today's food stores. (See Appendix B)

Supermarkets offer more than just food savings. They are excellent sources for first-aid supplies and pharmaceuticals. Ask the pharmacist for advice. He should be able to help you stock a functional first-aid kit, while keeping supplies to a minimum. They also know all about generic drugs. Many expensive brand name drugs have generic equivalents that are less than half the price of the brand name.

Upon reviewing the gear and grub, it certainly appears that some money needs to be spent for provisions. But backpacking offers a basic benefit that is hard to find in other types of vacations—free activities! Don't worry about packing any money. There are no stores, restaurants, gift shops, tourist traps, hotels, video games, movies, thrill rides, museums, or modern conveniences. Just think of all the cash you'll save. What a novel concept. Have fun and enjoy real life, without spending.

In the wilderness, entertainment is free, and you won't be bored. You can easily busy yourself with fishing, hiking, photography, mountaineering, wildlife study, exploring, meditating, camp-craft, campfire chats, primitive cooking, rock collecting, prospecting, sketching, swimming, playing active games with children, or by just enjoying some good old-fashioned R&R. Allow ample time to experience some of the freebies. What a welcome change from our hectic, money oriented, work-a-day world.

Scenery and aesthetics are also *no charge.* What price have you paid for a pleasing atmosphere in a fine restaurant? Yet in the backcountry, it is free and real. Sometimes it is a little too real when the weather or the bugs act up, but that's all part of the great outdoors.

Where fires are permitted, fuel is free. Firewood for warmth and cooking is available for the gathering. About the only way you'll have to pay for it is if you hire someone to rustle up some wood. Hmmm, that's not a bad idea if you're pressed for time, the fish are biting, and you can find someone gullible enough. I have yet to be so lucky.

Backpacking, what a deal! In fact it's the best darn deal for the money I can think of. The gear can be inexpensive or improvised, the food purchased at a supermarket, and activities are free. Hey, maybe that's why I like it so much. No, not really. It's not the economics of backpacking I thrive on, it's the sport itself. Backpacking is something different, meaningful, and wonderful to each soul.

Many happy trails....

Appendix A: Gear Checklist

Pocket Items
__ Waterproof matches
__ Knife
__ Compass
__ Snacks

__ _____

Individual Items
__ Sleeping bag
__ Sleeping pad
__ Water container
__ Flashlight
__ Toilet Tissue
__ Toothbrush
__ Comb
__ Insect repellent
__ Pencil & note cards
__ Extra socks
__ Extra shoes
__ Poncho
__ Plate, cup, & utensils
__ Medications

__ _____

Group Items
__ Tent or tarp
__ Rope
__ Map
__ First-aid supplies
__ Needle or sewing kit
__ Pot, pan, spatula
__ Stove

__ _____

Optional
__ Fishing gear
__ Camera
__ Saw
__ Pliers
__ Spade
__ Safety pin
__ Watch
__ Sunglasses
__ Mirror
__ Hand soap
__ Sunblock
__ Lip balm
__ Salt tablets
__ Bandanna
__ Gloves
__ Day pack
__ Stocking cap
__ Purification tablets
__ Purification pump
__ Candle
__ Whistle
__ Journal

__ _____

What to Wear
__ Wide brim hat
__ Collared shirt
__ T-shirt
__ Tight socks
__ Loose pants
__ Jacket or sweater
__ Hiking boots

__ _____

Appendix B: Menu Planner

BREAKFAST

Entrée	Side Dish	Beverage
Bacon	Hash browns	Hot choc.
Sausage	Toaster pastry	Pwdr. milk
Eggs (med.)	English muffin	Pwdr. juice
Powdered eggs	Dried fruit	Tea
Pancakes	Jam / syrup	Coffee
Instant oatmeal	Granola	Water
Fresh fish	Granola bar	

DINNER

Entree	Side Dish	Dessert
Tuna Helper (fish)	Mashed potatoes	Pudding
Fresh fish	Hash browns	Dried fruit
Steak	Potato pancakes	Cake (mix)
Hot dogs	Seasoned noodles	Muffins
Beef log/stick	Soup mix	Cheesecake
Taco w/cheese	Ramen soup	
Dried beef	Rice	see snacks
Smoked fish	Dried beans	
Smoked turkey	Macaroni & cheese	
Spaghetti	Pasta salad	

SNACKS

Peanuts	Beef jerky	Raisins
Cashews	Beef stick	Dried fruit
Sunflower seeds	Candy (wrapped)	Crackers
Mixed nuts	String cheese	Gum
Trail mix	Marshmallows	Cheese
Granola bars	Pretzels	Chips
Cookies	Potato sticks	Popcorn

About the Author

Jeffrey Probst is a lifelong resident of the state of Utah. His favorite place to backpack is the High Uinta Mountains of Utah, where he might be found once the snow retreats. Fishing, solitude, and photography are his main reasons for packing into the backcountry.

Still a kid at heart, he enjoys talking about his mountain retreats, and inspiring others to enjoy similar experiences. He loves to get kids (old ones too) excited about fishing the backcountry by relating some of his better fishing trips to them. Fishing stories are not the only ones he tells, as he usually has a strange but *sometimes* true tale reserved for the evening campfire.

www.ingramcontent.com/pod-product-compliance
Lightning Source LLC
Chambersburg PA
CBHW031320040426

42443CB00005B/155